THE SPIRIT OF SIMPLE LIVING

Simple Caring

SHARON HANBY-ROBIE

Guideposts®

CARMEL, NEW YORK 10512

Acknowledgments

Every attempt has been made to credit the sources of copyrighted material used in this book. If any such acknowledgment has been inadvertently omitted or miscredited, receipt of such information would be appreciated.

All material that originally appeared in *Daily Guideposts* is reprinted with permission.

Scripture quotations marked (AMP) are taken from *The Amplified Bible,* © 1965 by Zondervan Publishing House. All rights reserved.

Scripture quotations marked (ESV) are taken from *The Holy Bible, English Standard Version.* Copyright © 2001 by Crossway Bibles, a division of Good News Publishers.

Scripture quotations marked (KJV) are taken from *The King James Version of the Bible.*

Scripture quotations marked (MSG) are taken from *The Message.* Copyright © 1993, 1994, 1995, 1996, 2000, 2001, 2002 by Eugene H. Peterson.

Scripture quotations marked (NIV) are taken from *The Holy Bible, New International Version.* Copyright © 1973, 1978, 1984 International Bible Society. Used by permission of Zondervan Bible Publishers.

Scripture quotations marked (NLT) are taken from the *Holy Bible*, New Living Translation. Copyright © 1996. Used by permission of Tyndale House Publishers, Inc., Wheaton, Illinois 60189. All rights reserved.

Scripture quotations marked (RSV) are taken from the *Revised Standard Version of the Bible.* Copyright © 1946, 1952, 1971 by Division of Christian Education of the National Council of Churches in Christ in the U.S.A. Used by permission.

www.guideposts.org
1-800-431-2344
Guideposts Books & Inspirational Media Division
Developmental Editors: Cristine Bolley and Deb Strubel
Cover design by Diane Bonder
Interior design by Cindy LaBreacht
Photo © Royalty-Free/Corbis
Typeset by Nancy Tardi
Printed in the United States of America

Contents

Introduction

I read a story about an old man who was stranded on a cold winter night. His beard was glazed with frost and his body was numb before he finally heard horses coming. He watched anxiously as several horsemen passed without slowing down to help him.

As the last rider rode by, the old man caught his eye and asked, "Sir, would you mind giving me a ride to the other side?" The rider helped him onto his horse graciously. He sensed the old man was half frozen, so he decided to take him all the way home rather than simply across the stream, even though it was a couple of miles out of his way. As they rode, the horseman asked the old man, "Why didn't you ask one of the others to help you? I was the last one. What if I'd refused?"

The old man replied, "Son, I've lived a long while and I think I know people pretty well. When I looked into their eyes I saw no concern for me at all. I knew it would be useless to ask. But when I looked into your eyes, I saw kindness and compassion."

As he was leaving the old man at the door of his home, the rider looked up and said a prayer, "May I never get too busy with my own affairs that I fail to respond to the needs of others." And with that, President Thomas Jefferson turned and directed his horse back toward the White House.

That story is the perfect example of the attitude of caring. Honest caring is not done with any hope of being rewarded. It combines goodness, kindliness and graciousness. Caring is the characteristic of Christ, a fruit of the Spirit and a distinctive trait of those who belong to Christ. It is God at work *in* you. He is the great motivator, enabler and empowerer.

We are living in a time of tremendous cultural change, and the demonstration of the Spirit of the Lord is as important as ever. The attributes of love, compassion, cooperation and forgiveness seem to be in short supply. In a "me first" world, it's easy to become callous to one another.

Philippians 2:3–4 cautions us to do nothing out of selfish ambition or vain conceit but in humility consider others better than ourselves. That is the key to simply caring in the way Christ has cared for us. Just as He accepted each of us, so too must we accept others. We cannot truly care for another unless we have first accepted him or her, faults and all. Whether we are caring for a parent, a patient or a friend, true caring is prompted by love.

So take a tip from Thomas Jefferson, and carefully saddle up your horse for the long journey of a lifetime of caring.

—*Sharon Hanby-Robie*

PART ONE

Caring Is the Heartbeat of Love

ALL THE ADMIRABLE VIRTUES OF CHARACTER, such as kindness, gentleness and patience, are diluted if a person's motivation is not based on caring about others. Caring is a synonym for love, and without it our lives are quickly drained of purpose. Because caring is at the heart of every good relationship, thinking about how we care about others is a valuable investment of our time. Once we understand how much God cares for us, it is easy to care for others. God generously blesses those who care for others so that they can continue to be caregivers. Because of God's principle of sowing and reaping, we find that the simple acts of caring create a life-giving cycle that returns love to us when we need it ourselves.

What Is Caring?

Therefore, as God's chosen people, holy and dearly loved,
clothe yourselves with compassion, kindness, humility,
gentleness and patience.

—COLOSSIANS 3:12 (NIV)

It is impossible to write a book about "caring" without first defining what caring means. Most simply put, caring is feeling or giving interest or having concern for someone. Its active expression is tending to someone's needs. But as I researched this topic, I discovered that merely defining the word is insufficient because caring is also the core of all good character traits. For example, we cannot be trustworthy unless we care. We cannot be respectful unless we care. We won't be responsible unless we care. It's difficult to be fair if we don't care. It's impossible to have integrity unless we do care.

Caring is often listed as one of the essential character traits that we admire in others. Without incorporating the core element of caring into the other traits, a person's actions will seem void of selfless compassion. Without the component of caring, we can "act fairly" without being fair. Caring must be a key ingredient of all our other personality traits; caring is what gives value to human relationships.

The epigraph of this chapter, Colossians 3:12, contains five great Christian virtues that provide a good description of the word *caring*. This verse says we are to clothe ourselves with (1) compassion, (2) kindness, (3) humility, (4) gentleness and (5) patience—all together, they manifest love. We cannot truly care without love for others. Since God's Word lists these five virtues as holy qualities in His people, it seems important to consider the value of each one.

A close study of *compassion* betokens pity and tenderness expressed toward those who are suffering. The Greek word used in this verse for *kindness* is *chrestotes*. Its root *charis* denotes that which causes joy or pleasure, that which creates delight in the recipient or observer. It was used especially to describe favors done without expectation of something in return. Honest caring is given without any hope of being rewarded.

Humility and *gentleness* are related terms: humility denotes a humble disposition; gentleness is the opposite of pride and self-assertiveness. Humility, with its counterpart of gentleness, is the special mark of one who has a delicate consideration for the rights and feelings of others. Humility with gentleness is the characteristic of Christ, a fruit of the Spirit and a distinctive trait of those who belong to Christ. When we care for others with gentleness, we do so without judging them. And withholding judgment can be difficult, especially when we think someone has brought suffering on himself by his own actions or decisions. If we are to care as Christ cared, then we must be humble and not feel compelled to lecture or give our own self-assertive opinions as a precondition of our caring.

Patience denotes the self-restraint that enables one to bear injury and insult without resorting to retaliation. This too can be hard because sometimes the person we are caring for can be difficult or even hurtful.

CARING IS A RESPONSE

Recently, a family member was admitted to the hospital with a life-threatening illness. She is only twenty-one. As the days led to weeks with no relief or hope of resolving her illness, her attitude deteriorated. Soon her frustration took on the form of angry verbalization toward anyone entering her room. Under the circumstances, patience was the only good response to have toward her. She was scared, in pain and feeling hopeless. She needed the grace of our patience. Her words simply expressed her emotions and shouldn't have been taken personally.

Caring is both a noun and a verb. We can say we "care" about many things, meaning we feel interest or concern. We can care whether or not our favorite team wins, but simply caring does not assist our team in winning the game. This is a passive form of caring. The active form of caring for someone is to *do* something to help. Real caring is always an action carried out by one person in regard for another. Caring does not require us to be emotionally involved, but it does require that we identify with the other and consider that person to be valuable or important enough to care about. When we open our hearts to the pain and suffering of others we can feel compassion toward them. Compassion allows us to feel the pain of another and calls our hearts to help.

Living a life of caring involves all other relationship values. Caring is only developed when we acknowledge its correlation to trust, honesty, humility and patience. Ultimately, caring makes Christ's presence and grace a living reality, and that can take on different forms, depending on the situation.

Sometimes caring is simply *what* we do—we offer care. Other times, it is as a *result* of what we do. In the end, both the caregiver and the recipient are changed. For example, you smile at me, I feel something and smile back. You listen to me and I feel more trusting of you. As the result of what we do and what happens, we are changed, just as Guideposts writer Daniel Schantz discovered as he waited in line at the post office:

> The post office.
> Long lines.
> I'm in a hurry.
> My turn at last, but a bony, shabby, old woman pushes ahead of me.
> My face feels hot, but I say nothing.
> Her transaction is long and complicated.
> I fidget. I fume. I sigh.
> Patiently, the clerk explains the procedure to her.
> Her eyes seem puzzled.
> He goes over it again.
> I check my watch and grind my teeth.
> The clerk goes over it a third time.
> Still, she only shakes her head.
> I want to scream. I've been here seven minutes. Or years.
> Suddenly, the lady puts her palms to her face and begins to sob like a little child.
> My anger vanishes. Pity fills me.

Defeated, the old woman gathers up her papers and shuffles away. I feel an impulse to offer to help her, but it comes too late. She is gone, through the door.

I send a silent prayer after her. I make a vow: Today, I will try to remember that there are more important things in life than speed. One of them is compassion.

SIMPLICITY MADE SIMPLE

CARING TAKES PRACTICE. Caring is a potential in every human being. Unfortunately, some people develop their potential and others do not. Caring is not an instinctual reaction to need. It's something we must experiment with, develop and make a regular habit.

TAKE CARE OF YOURSELF FIRST. We must be secure in ourselves in order to reach out to another. To be secure, we must first have the resources and the ability to respond effectively to our own problems. I have a friend who cannot help others because she simply doesn't have the capability to help herself. Her own insecurity makes her too vulnerable emotionally to help others. Sadly, because she is fearful, she is not even able to "hear" about another's woes without being overwhelmed. To be caring, we must not be fearful.

BE ETHICAL. Caring is the heart of ethics. It is not possible to be truly ethical, or live with integrity, unless you have a genuine concern for others. Yet, there are people who consider themselves ethical and still lack a caring attitude toward others. Michael Josephson, founder of Josephson Institute of

Ethics and the Character Counts youth education initiative, says, "They [people who are not genuinely concerned with the welfare of others] rarely feel an obligation to be honest, loyal, fair or respectful except insofar as it is prudent for them to do so."

ACT WITHOUT THOUGHT FOR THE OUTCOME of the act. Caring involves the assumption that the other person can be helped. But it does not assure that the other person *will* be helped.

CARING INVOLVES DESIRE, MOTIVATION AND INCLINATION. If you care for someone, you feel a desire or inclination toward them. That is different from being given responsibility for another's welfare, which can result in caretaking that is perfunctory or grudging. A core element of caring is being "responsive." The one who is caring must be sufficiently engrossed in the other to listen to him or her with an attitude that warms and comforts.

> Dear Lord, I understand that my life will be empty
> if I don't love and care about the welfare of others.
> So I give You my heart and ask that You fill it
> with Your love, and I gladly give both my heart and my
> hands to the service of others on Your behalf. Amen.

Why and When We Do Care

We love because he first loved us.

—1 JOHN 4:19 (NIV)

In my younger days, I went out on a first date with a guy named Mack. On our way to the movie theater we passed a motorist with a flat tire. Without hesitation, Mack turned the car around and headed to help. Changing the tire took about a half hour—by which time we were late for the movie. But that didn't matter. What mattered, at least to me, was how powerfully I was affected by this simple act of kindness. If I had been traveling by myself, I never would have stopped, for obvious reasons—I'm a female and too petite to be of much help in changing a tire. But nonetheless, I was impressed at how quickly and selflessly Mack acted. He never thought to ask me whether or not I minded if we were late for the movie. Helping a stranger in distress was just a natural thing for Mack to do.

But such acts of kindness are not natural for everyone. In fact, psychologists have discovered that certain factors affect whether or not we offer help. Some of these factors have to do with the environment, that is, the situation in which we find ourselves, while others pertain to our individual characteristics and our state of mind. One of the more interesting, and I think frightening, facts is that the more people there are who witness someone in need, the less likely anyone is to help. Many studies have been published on this topic. Researchers found that any given individual is more likely to come to another person's aid if he or she believes no one else can do so. Why? Because when there is a crowd, we may assume someone else has already done something. Or, if no one else is responding we may conclude that the situation doesn't really warrant intervention. Third, we fear appearing foolish in the eyes of others if it turns out no help was actually needed. Fourth, the duty to act is shared by everyone present, which diminishes the responsibility and thereby reduces our own obligation and ultimate blame.

Another interesting study found that *contented* people are more likely to extend themselves to others. The better we feel, the more willing we are to help. The more we help, the better we feel. Also, if someone is sad, she will feel sympathetic sadness or guilt toward the other and be more likely to help. However, if someone is angry, he probably won't help. Another significant factor is our level of self-awareness or indulgence. If we are thinking about the misfortune of the other person, we will help. But if we are preoccupied with our own state of mind, we won't.

Besides our mood and state of mind, there are two other factors that affect our willingness to help: whether or not we feel competent to help, and whether or not we feel guilty over something else we recently did. When we feel incompetent, we feel helpless. Healthy self-esteem or confidence is likely to make someone more caring and helpful. But obligation or indebtedness can work too. Feeling obligated to help someone is a powerful motivator. If someone feels responsible, even by default, they more readily offer help. For example, simply being present and witnessing someone being mugged can make you feel obligated enough to respond.

But there is hope for all of us to be more caring regardless of circumstances. It's the truth of 1 John 4:19, "We love because he first loved us."

WE CARE BECAUSE GOD CARES FOR US

Although studies have shown that there is virtually no connection between religious affiliation or belief and extending help or care to others, Christians have a motivation that is distinct—the love of Christ. Any Christian can answer the question "Why should I care?" with the facts from two thousand years ago when God identified Himself fully with our humanness. Kenneth C. Haugk, author of *Christian Caregiving—A Way of Life*, wrote, "He sent His Son into the world to live and breathe, to suffer and love, to minister and care—and finally to die. Through His church Jesus continues to extend His ministry of love and care for people. The love of Christ is powerful and dynamic. It is not just a good feeling: it is the basic motivation for all Christian caring."

Christians offer care that is distinctive not in *what* we do, but in *why* we do it. As Christians we have a clear religious sense of identity as a caregiver. We realize that we are an extension of Christ's ministry and we are empowered by His love. Christ's love shows, no matter how insignificant the actual act of caring is, as demonstrated in writer Patricia Lorenz's story about her own family:

The big yellow school bus swallowed up Andrew as I dashed for the front stoop to wave vigorously, blow him a kiss, then end the routine with more wild waving as the bus ground forward.

"Why do you do that silly waving routine every morning, Mom?" asked fifteen-year-old Julie.

"Every single day since Andrew started kindergarten last year, he has left the house with the words, 'Wave to me when the bus comes . . . and don't forget the kiss part.'"

"You didn't wave to me every day when I was in first grade," reminded fourteen-year-old Michael.

"That's because you had your two older sisters with you. Andrew needs to know he's not alone when he leaves. One of these days he'll get on the bus and forget even to look for me. But for now, I *like* feeling needed."

You know what? After that conversation Julie started giving me a quick kiss on the cheek as she bounded out the door for the bus and Michael made sure to holler, "Bye, Mom!" even if I was in the bathroom getting ready for work. I like the "leaving routines" our family has every morning that tie us together with a string of love and caring.

I've read that it takes seven days to make a habit. This week, why not form a new good-morning/good-bye habit with the people you love?

Just as love bound the Lorenz family together in caring, so too does Christ's love bind us all as a family that simply cares.

SIMPLICITY MADE SIMPLE

MAKE THE FIRST MOVE. Next time you see someone in need, don't wait to find out if someone else is going to respond. Remember, the longer you hesitate, the less likely you are to help.

You are not alone. Remember that as a person of faith, you have a special assurance and strength in the power of God. You do not have to rely solely on your own resources. **PUT ON AN ATTITUDE OF HUMILITY** and submission and you will soon find yourself reaching out to others with a new desire to serve.

DON'T FEEL COMPELLED OR OBLIGED TO SHARE YOUR MOTIVATION. It is not necessary to always divulge our personal motives with the one we are caring for. Sometimes it's appropriate and other times it is not. In fact, it may even cause the other person to believe you think you are superior. So be careful. Haugk in *Christian Caregiving* suggests "[e]valuating the other person's needs. Make sure when you share your basic motivation, it is what the other person needs to hear, not simply what you want them to hear. Your ultimate motivation for caring may well be Jesus. He provides purpose and power so that your caring relationships are transformed by His love. Knowing this will affect your identity, attitude, confidence and perspective as a caregiver."

CARING DOESN'T REQUIRE FONDNESS. Samuel Johnson said, "Kindness is in our power, even when fondness is not." Christ said we are to love even our enemies. I wonder what would happen if we showered them with kindness and caring? We do not need to feel warmly toward someone we do not like. We care because we should—regardless of how we feel. Some call this *ethical* caring. The point is simply to act.

CREATE A CIRCLE OF CARING. The circular nature of caring produces a cycle of caring. When we do something "as a result of experiencing caring" rather than "in return for caring," caring becomes unconditional and circular—the caring simply continues.

> Lord, it's amazing that You care so much for me
> that You know how many hairs are on my head!
> Help me to notice even the small details in the lives
> of others so that I can encourage them to
> celebrate Your presence in their lives. Amen.

How We Show That We Care

"For whatever is in your heart
determines what you say."

—MATTHEW 12:34 (NLT)

Caring seems like a simple concept, but it gets a bit complex when you dig deeper into the whole idea of caring. Psychologists Larry Crabb and Dan Allender give some interesting insight in their book *Encouragement—The Key to Caring*. They say, "Encouragement, as we understand it, is more than acquiring a new set of skills. It is the fruit of a self-examined heart and a compassionate, discerning sensitivity to the need of others." In other words, we can only produce encouraging words when we have humble and loving hearts.

True encouragement is prompted by love and requires involvement. It starts as soon as we encounter another person—right then we have the option of engaging or not. For example, you pass an old acquaintance on the street. It's obvious by her appearance that something is wrong. You realize that this is a great opportunity to offer encouragement, but you must first recognize that the person may find it difficult to be vulnerable and tell you what is troubling her. She may think that you wouldn't care about her dilemma, or she may be afraid of being rejected.

Your first words must give the clear message that you are interested in whatever she has to say and that you will accept her regardless of what she says. To do that, you must become an active listener. Active listening requires concentrated effort so you can be aware of those nuances that tell more than most people are willing to reveal with their words. Slumped shoulders, deep sighs, and moist eyes deliver a loud and clear message that words may not convey.

Encouragement depends on *accepting* a person whose needs and faults lie exposed. Acceptance is a key principle for being an encourager—it assures a person that he or she will not be rejected. We must also be understanding, but this does not require that we give advice. In fact, sometimes understanding is better than advice. This is especially true with husbands and wives, and men and women in general. Men naturally want to fix things. But women, more often than not, simply want a sensitive ear.

When we are too quick to respond with solutions, it can appear as though we are demeaning the other person by saying there is a simple solution to the problem. Rather than giving advice, an encourager can help someone clarify what is happening and how he or she is feeling. Quiet listening combined with sensitive probing is a simple way to show we care.

SOMEONE MAY BE HAVING A BAD DAY

People who need encouragement also need to have their own sense of value reinforced. Because we were designed by God to be relational beings, we need acceptance and we need to know that others value us. Our greatest fears are *rejection* and *insignificance*. Words that address these needs and fears.

Chuck Wall, founder of the World Kindness Movement, explained kindness this way: "An act that positively influences the life of both giver and the receiver is a kindness. It doesn't have to cost money or be difficult to perform. It can be spontaneous (random) or premeditated. It can be as simple as a smile or a thank-you, and as complicated as starting a nonprofit organization to benefit those in need."

Guideposts writer Shari Smyth wrote about how a simple act by strangers significantly affected the life of her daughter:

> When my daughter Sanna told me she had found a job as a waitress, I waited with dread and hope to hear how her first day went. Success was crucial. Newly out of drug and alcohol rehab, she was on the mend in spirit, body and mind. That night, after her first day, she phoned me. "Something awful happened at work," she said.
>
> My stomach churned. "Tell me about it, Sanna."
>
> "I was carrying a pitcher of iced tea to my very first table when I had a panic attack. I began shaking and sweating. I put the pitcher down and ran to the ladies' room, praying. I felt God telling me to go out and try again. So I did. The couple at that table was there. They'd waited a long time."
>
> "What happened?" I asked, gripping the phone.
>
> "Well, I started pouring the iced tea for them, and I was so nervous I spilled it all over the table."
>
> By this time I could scarcely breathe. "Go on, Sanna."
>
> "Here's the thing, though, Mom. They were so nice. The man said, 'Honey, don't be afraid. We're just folk like you.'

The woman took my hand and told me to take all the time I needed, that they weren't in a hurry. So I slowed down, took deep breaths and got through it. The rest of the night went fine. I think I'm gonna make it, Mom."

From the bottom of my heart, I thank this anonymous couple who showed mercy to their "inept" waitress, never dreaming how crucial their response was.

God is so amazing. He knew how much Sanna was going to need encouragement that night so He sent a couple of earth-angels to do the job.

SIMPLICITY MADE SIMPLE

ENGAGE ALL ASPECTS OF ENCOURAGEMENT: dignity, respect, compassion and humility. If you have all of these things for yourself, you will then be able to share them with others.

Learn to listen actively. Active listening requires that we be other-directed and also resist projecting our own feelings and ideas onto someone else. We must be nondefensive. When we are busy protecting or justifying our own opinions or actions, it is difficult to focus on the other person. **LISTEN AS A RECEIVER AND NOT AS A CRITIC.** The last thing someone in need of care deserves is criticism. Give your undivided attention and look into the eyes of the person who is speaking.

SAY YOU ARE SORRY and mean it. I heard Norman Corwin, professor and journalist, on National Public Radio's *This I Believe* series. He said that years ago while watching a baseball game on television, he saw Orel

Hershiser, who was pitching for the Dodgers, throw a fastball that hit a batter. The camera was close-up on Hershiser, and Corwin could read his lips as he mouthed, "I'm sorry." The batter, taking first base, nodded to the pitcher in a friendly way and the game went on. Those two words—I'm sorry—said everything good about Hershiser, the batter and baseball. It was a simple common courtesy that made a lasting impression for Corwin to remember all these years later.

DEMONSTRATE CARING EVERY DAY. You can show that you care by simple acts of kindness. For example, help people move—packing up or unpacking and putting away. Call someone to carpool whenever possible. Call and offer to babysit someone's children for the day without being asked. Hold the door open for the person behind you at the bank, grocery store, anywhere.

ACTIVELY SEEK OUT OPPORTUNITIES to assist others. Give clear signals that show you are accessible and friendly. Learn and practice conflict resolution and reconciliation. Simply acknowledge others' efforts, successes, contributions and kindnesses whenever you notice.

SHOW YOUNG PEOPLE YOU CARE by simply noticing them. Acknowledge them, learn their names and look them in the eyes when you talk to them. Be nice, be honest, be yourself. Ask for their opinions, listen to their stories and hug them. Believe in them, expect the best from them and respect them. Help them learn from their mistakes without criticizing.

PRACTICE THESE WAYS OF CARING: Apologize when you have made a mistake or overreacted. When you are stressed or unavailable, explain that it is a condition of life and that you do not mean to ignore the other person. Help others discover what has meaning and purpose for them. Give lots of compliments. Listen and learn from what others have to say. Give your undivided attention. Praise others for their courage.

Don't forget to **CARE FOR THOSE YOU LOVE**. Sometimes your schedule can make the day a virtual haze. You may unintentionally neglect the art of communication in your important relationships. Expressing your love and care on a daily basis can be as simple as sincerely saying "I love you," at least once a day. Have dinner together as often as you can. If you have loved ones whom you don't see every day, remember to schedule a lunch or dinner with them at least once a month. Mark the date on your calendar to make sure it happens.

Reciprocate the caring. **ALLOW OTHERS TO CARE FOR YOU** when you are in need. Like all good things, the idea is to pass it on. When we do, we encourage others to grow in their ability to care and reap the rewards that caring gives.

> Lord, I would like to be an "earth-angel" today.
> When someone is speaking to me, help me to focus
> on his or her needs and enable me to be a source of
> encouragement for everyone I meet. Amen.

It's All in the Doing

Do not conform any longer to the pattern of this world,
but be transformed by the renewing of your mind.
Then you will be able to test and approve what
God's will is—his good, pleasing and perfect will.

—ROMANS 12:2 (NIV)

Recently, I met with a new interior design client. It didn't take long to figure out that the new client was in a transition. The furniture in her house gave it away. On one side of the room was a pretty rattan and glass dining table with a beautiful floral-patterned oriental carpet beneath—very feminine. On the other side, along with a chair and sofa, were two heavy oak tables—not very feminine.

When I commented that it appeared that she was in transition, she replied, "I went through a divorce."

"Aha . . . been there, done that," was my response. I tried to offer her some assurance by relating something from a difficulty in my own past. "The good news is that as you come through this process you will emerge, step-by-step as the most beautiful butterfly ever. But this only happens if you are willing to go through the pain and the time of the process." There we stood, women at different stages of the same process.

I have watched several women go through the cocoon-to-butterfly transformation as a result of divorce or death of a spouse. But I have also seen a few examples of women who attempted to sidestep the process to avoid the pain. As a result, they have also missed the joy of experiencing change. The experience of divorce was the same, but the results were immensely different.

Helping people work through difficult times or resolve problems can be rewarding. But we must be careful that we don't focus solely on results. Focusing on results alone can hinder caring and can be counterproductive to the one we are caring for. For example, in helping someone get through a divorce, we might easily fall into the "results-oriented" goal of getting her out of the house and socializing with others. The fact of the matter may be that she is not yet emotionally ready for such a situation. Simply seeing happy couples together could cause her to break down and cry, leaving her even more emotionally hurt than before. We should instead focus on the *process* of preparing her to consider the possibility of socializing at some time in the future.

RENEWAL IS AN ENJOYABLE PROCESS

Romans 12:2 is about the ongoing process of renewing our minds. The process of healing is also an ongoing one. We cannot simply determine that our minds are renewed instantly. We must accept renewal as part of our daily mission, always going back in our thoughts to our original commitment to God and reaffirming it. This requires dedication and discernment. In going through this process, we find delight in doing God's will. There is an intimate connection between certifying the will of God and making oneself a living sacrifice. There is joy in the process of living daily according to His will, despite the fact that we will never accomplish the goal of a perfectly renewed mind.

Overemphasis on results can slow down healing and growth. It's all a matter of properly placed expectations. As caregivers, we should encourage those who need our support to share their fears rather than expecting them to ignore their feelings. We should let them know that it is okay to grieve, to cry and to be angry, rather than expecting them to simply change their thinking. Ultimately, we must recognize that the primary results are those that God accomplishes in our lives.

As I spoke with this new client, it was with confidence that we had arrived at the same understanding at the end of the process—we no longer needed to know where God was leading—we simply needed to trust Him. That is the best result. But neither of us could have gotten to it if we had not gone through the whole journey.

Susan Jeffers, psychologist and author of *Embracing Uncertainty,* says, "Once you surrender to the fact you are unable to control the uncertainty, you will at last be able to breathe a sigh of relief." As we care for others we can assure them that while they are sincerely engaged in the process, God will help them bring it to completion (Philippians 1:6).

We cannot control the outcome, but we can promote the process. We must rely on God for results. Only He can provide healing. That truth frees us to give more abundantly and to focus more fully on today—leaving the future to Him.

Guideposts writer Arthur M. Powell wrote about how his grandma taught him the process for taking action and leaving the results to God.

One Sunday morning in 1964 as we left the Abyssinian Baptist Church, Grandma Powell stopped on the sidewalk, lifted my chin and, using my middle name, said, "Maxwell, you have got to do the Word."

She pointed back to the old stone church. "You heard what the preacher said—to pray, to ask the Lord for guidance and protection? Well, it won't do you much good unless you . . ."

She took my arm and directed my attention to a man lolling against a lamppost. "See that man? He's always bragging about his big plans but he never does anything.

"Talk is easy," she continued. "It's the doing that counts. God tells us to be doers of his Word and not just hearers. Remember, Maxwell, Monday doing is better than Sunday talking."

Years later, Arthur Maxwell Powell joined the military and eventually found himself in Saudi Arabia during the Persian Gulf War.

I was scared—I admit it. I was in the communications ground crew with the F–117A Stealth Fighter Wing. Our radar-evading aircraft were the only manned fighters that dared to invade central Baghdad.

My fear in the Gulf War? It didn't last long. All I had to remember was to do the Word of Psalm 91: "The Lord . . . is my refuge . . . Thou shalt not be afraid for the terror by night; nor for the arrow that flieth by day." I did my job, trusting God to take care of me.

The same is true for us as caregivers—to simply do the job God has asked us to do and then leave the rest to Him.

S I M P L I C I T Y   M A D E   S I M P L E

Encourage growth by encouraging those in your care to allow events to change them. God is in charge, and all that we experience passes through His hand first. Therefore, not only can we get through this experience, but we can be made better by it if we are willing to grow. In her article "Recovery as a Self-Directed Process of Healing and Transformation," Patricia E. Deegan, psychologist and herself a survivor of a traumatic experience, said, "Recovery is often defined conservatively as returning to a stable baseline or former level of functioning. However, many people, including myself, have experienced **RECOVERY AS A TRANSFORMATIVE PROCESS** in which the old self is gradually let go of and a new sense of self emerges."[1]

Recognize that **PROCESS IS MORE IMPORTANT THAN OUTCOME**. Happiness is simply here and now, no matter where you are in the process. If you have a goal and you're dissatisfied until you achieve the end result, then happiness won't occur until you get there. And sometimes when the goal is achieved, its celebration lasts but a fleeting moment. It's better to not know where you are going, enjoy the ride and then be surprised by the destination when you get there, than to postpone happiness until certain goals are reached.

HELP OTHERS ENJOY TODAY. When the focus is only on future goals, people become absent from the present and miss opportunities for joy today. When a goal is not achieved, they often face setbacks. They may find themselves simply setting yet another goal that may be unachievable—which will only set them back further. Point out to them the good that you see in their lives right now.

CHANGE LIVES BY CHANGING ATTITUDES. A good deal of social psychological research concludes that through positive changes in attitudes, and actual behavior, you can affect future outcomes. You'll find that focusing on the processes involved in your goal-directed activities, rather than on favorable outcomes, will help you to achieve your goals. Unfortunately, many self-help books focus on goals and results rather than process, which sets you up to fail.

Lord, I realize that You are more interested in how we live than in what we achieve. I will trust You as I face the challenge of change, and I will encourage others to put their hope in You too. Your presence makes the process of being transformed a wonderful event in our lives. Amen.

What Caring Does for You and Others

Remember this:

Whoever sows sparingly will also reap sparingly,

and whoever sows generously will also reap generously.

—2 CORINTHIANS 9:6 (NIV)

We reap what we sow. When it comes to caring, it's simple: the more we care for others, the more they will care for us, and the better we feel. Tamara Traeder, coauthor of *Girlfriends,* says, "As we open up to others with our help, we find an expansiveness in our own lives and fulfillment in our actions. We find that even when we take time out to help someone else, everything else that we have to do gets done. As we focus on others' difficulties, we put our own problems into perspective. The truth is that no one is exempt from needing help; we all have problems at one time or another."

Douglas M. Lawson, author of *Give to Live*, says the benefits of caring are numerous: "The physical benefits include greater longevity, enhanced functioning of the immune system, and improved cardiovascular circulation and healthier sleep." He says the emotional benefits are "increased self-acceptance, reduced self-absorption and sense of isolation, increased ability to cope with crises and improved concentration and enjoyment of experiences." He also says the spiritual benefits are great too, such as "greater connectedness to God, more receptivity to spiritual guidance, sustained peace of mind, greater clarity about the meaning and purpose of life and an overall enhanced quality of life." Whew! And that's just a partial list of the benefits he enumerates in his book.

And there seem to be virtually no negative effects to giving, volunteering or simply caring for others. Just imagine how much better we would all feel if we took the time to care a little more about others.

CARING IS HURTING WHEN OTHERS FEEL PAIN

I read a story about how a young man learned to care about others from his mother. His mom gave a party for some of the kids in their neighborhood. In the course of the party, one of the girls started to sit down. A boy yanked the chair out from behind her and she fell to the floor. No injury, but it hurt and she cried. The boys laughed. A few days later, as this young man prepared to sit down for dinner, his mom yanked the chair away. He fell to the floor. Mom laughed. When he looked up at Mom wanting to know why she laughed, she reminded him how he and the other boys had laughed when the girl had fallen. If it was funny then, why wasn't it funny now? He got the point. Other people hurt like he did.

Just as important is the fact that there are good feelings and real pleasures when we know we have helped to make someone's life richer. But not all feelings associated with caring are comfortable. Caring when it is not possible to help can be painful. And sometimes caring necessitates "tough love." When that mother pulled the chair out from behind her son, she was teaching him to care. She taught him that other people could be hurt. This is important because care for another is often motivated by our assumption that they feel the same way we do. We imagine how they feel based upon our own emotions and experiences. People who have not been conditioned or socialized to have such empathy can be scary because they lack an important motivator to care, which leaves them insensitive and even callous.

Caring is also an essential ingredient for any long-term relationship to be loving. It is the glue that holds us together and motivates our willingness to work toward the well-being of all involved. My sister recently told me that one of the biggest lessons she has learned about relationships is that you can be right all the time, but you'll probably be lonely, or you can be agreeable and willing to compromise and have a happy, fulfilling relationship.

The patterns of our relationships reflect how much we care about the other person. This kind of caring grows out of the understanding and appreciation of those we love. And our caring becomes tailored specifically to the individuals within the relationship. The goal of caring in a loving relationship should be for the well-being of all. This includes oneself.

Leo Buscaglia, the "hugging" psychologist and author of *Bus Nine to Paradise: A Loving Voyage*, says, "Each of us sooner or later realizes that our relationships with others require giving of ourselves—not only of our time, but our sincere and caring involvement as well. Too often we close the book on the many who need us by allotting just so much of ourselves, and end by being miserly with what should be the easiest and least expensive thing to give—ourselves." That's sad because one of the most rewarding experiences is helping others.

Studies show that owning pets or having plants promotes a longer and healthier life. Why? Because they require you to care for something besides yourself. Amazing. But I have seen this firsthand. Years ago, a friend of mine named Adelaide suddenly became a widow. She was emotionally devastated. She had never even gone to the grocery store alone. After three years, she was still struggling to come through the grief process. I made the decision to get her a puppy—to give her a reason to get out of bed in the morning.

I acquired the pup two months before Christmas and spent those months training him while Adelaide assumed the puppy was mine. She was shocked and a bit frightened to find him under her tree on Christmas morning. But I had a hunch it would be on target for her, and fortunately I was right. It changed her life. That little pup could not survive without her and she knew that. Caring for him gave her purpose and got her involved in the process of living again.

When we focus on something other than ourselves, not only do our lives improve, but we also make a difference in others' lives as well. Scott Harrison wrote for Guideposts about an experience he had with his young son:

> My son Chris was standing beside our bed at two in the morning. "What's wrong?" I asked groggily. "Why aren't you in bed?"
>
> His lips quivered. "My ear hurts a lot, Dad, and I can't sleep."
>
> Only five years old, he looked even younger standing in

the darkness. He had never chanced the dark hallway between our bedrooms before, so this must have been serious.

That afternoon, his pediatrician had started him on antibiotics for an ear infection. As I tucked Chris back in bed, I knew we'd just have to wait until the medication took effect. Feeling helpless, I bowed my head and prayed that the Lord would relieve my brave young son of his pain.

His small voice interrupted me. "It's okay Dad. I know how tired you are. You don't have to stay with me." I looked up to protest that I wasn't falling asleep, that I was just praying. Chris stared at me earnestly while he said, "Besides, it doesn't hurt quite as much now."

By focusing on me, not on the throbbing ear, his pain already seemed less. A few minutes later Chris was sleeping peacefully.

When something in my life hurts me—a misunderstanding with a friend, a promotion that doesn't materialize, the loss of a beloved pet—I'm going to remember what Chris taught me and focus my attention on the problems of others until my own hurt lessens.

SIMPLICITY MADE SIMPLE

GIVE AWAY SOME LOVE. As Leo Buscaglia says, "Love isn't love until it is given away. Until it's manifested through some caring act, love is nothing more than a very good idea—only an idea, a simple word, a notion in abstract.

There is something for each of us to do. We become truly human at the moment when we reach out to help someone." As men and women of faith we can offer God's love to others. For some, it may be the first time they ever experience perfect and unconditional love that only God can give. With God's love comes peace. Such peace is not merely the absence of hostility or a state of inner contentment, but rather it is the peace expressed by the Hebrew word *shalom*. Protestant scholar Walter Bruegemann said the following regarding shalom: "The central vision of world history in the Bible is that all of creation is one, every creature in community with every other, living in harmony and security toward the joy and well-being of every other creature . . . Shalom is the substance of the biblical vision of one community embracing all creation."[2]

Make the world a better place. It is essential for us to **RELATE IN CONSTRUCTIVE, CARING WAYS** to the world by helping or bringing pleasure to others. Such caring is necessary if we are to avoid being a heartless society. This morning as our little group of four women was getting ready to go into exercise class, one of the gals commented on how she had not had a good night's sleep and was in a rotten mood. After we laughed, we encouraged her to simply decide that no matter how she felt, she was going to be nice to everyone she came in contact with. That single act of determination will make a difference for those she meets today. Rather than scowling and huffing, she will be smiling— and we all know that smiles are contagious.

REACH OUT BEYOND YOUR COMFORT ZONE and forgive. Forgiving someone does not require that they become "forgivable," but rather that they are able to accept forgiveness and grace from God and others. I can think of many people who found themselves caring for a loved one with whom they had unresolved and unforgiven issues. One friend in particular cared for her father during his last days on earth. Years before there had been a bitter fight that had never been resolved. It had clearly hardened the relationship—as well as their love for each other. My friend, realizing that this was probably her last opportunity to bring healing, decided that forgiving her father was necessary for both of them. Her willingness to forgive her father gave him the ability to also forgive her and wholeheartedly love her during those last days simply because he received love and forgiveness first. As we learned from experiencing 1 John 4:19, we love because He first loved us.

Thank You for the capacity to care, even when caring is painful. Help me to know what to do when doing something is needed, and help me cope with my helplessness when nothing can be done. But most of all, cleanse me from the sin of apathy, for I would rather have a heart like Yours than to miss out on the reward of simply caring for others. Amen.

PART TWO

Caring Is a State of Mind

THE PSYCHOLOGY OF CARING BEGINS with healthy self-respect. It is easier to care for others when we are not focused on our own insecurities. Caring about others is an outlook that can be taught from one generation to the next. Children who watch caring adults will become responsible caregivers themselves. Following Christ's example keeps us in a frame of mind to actively nurture compassion for others. In this section, we will discuss how to fully engage in the selfless act of caring for others, and to quickly forgive those who may offend us. There is no room for bitterness or resentment if we are seriously trying to follow Christ's example of loving others. Instead, we must continue to make our best effort to stay connected to those for whom we care by keeping lines of communication open and honest. Then we will clearly see God's reward for those who care for others.

How We Learn the Process
of Caring

When he saw the crowds, he had compassion on them,

because they were harassed and helpless,

like sheep without a shepherd.

—MATTHEW 9:36 (NIV)

The great life of Christ is our model for living a compassionate and caring life. In fact, Christ's compassion was so deep and beyond anything anyone had ever experienced before, that a new word was coined, *spagkhnozomai*, simply to describe the compassion of Christ. Its root is in the word *splanchnon*, which literally translates to *intestines*. C. H. Spurgeon explained this way, "I suppose that when our Saviour looked upon certain sights, those who watched Him closely perceived that His internal agitation was very great, His emotions were very deep, and then His face betrayed it, His eyes gushed like founts with tears, and you saw that His big heart was ready to burst with pity for the sorrow upon which His eyes were gazing. He was moved with compassion. His whole nature was agitated with commiseration for the sufferers before him."[3]

There is a saying, "People do not care how much we know, until they know how much we care." So how can we learn to be compassionate like Christ? Modern medical and social scientists agree that a person's pattern of generosity and caring is established during the first four or five years of life. A parent's example is especially important in determining whether or not a child becomes a compassionate adult. Compassionate people feel the feelings of others, but compassion doesn't necessarily come naturally. Some theologians believe that original sin tainted our ability to be naturally compassionate. Regardless, it doesn't take much observation to realize that most little children are self-centered, willful and even manipulative. A two-year-old wants what she wants, when she wants it, regardless of anyone else's needs. Yet, the same child, in another mood, might notice some other child crying and bring her a favorite toy or blanket to comfort her. This awareness of another's pain and the desire to bring comfort is the foundation of a compassionate heart. We may not be born completely compassionate, but we certainly have the seed of Christ's compassion in us and that can be nurtured.

Although little children may be naturally self-centered, by the age of three, they can begin to identify and empathize with the complex emotions of others. They learn by both word and example to be generous and caring. If parents verbally encourage sharing but they themselves act selfishly, the child will be confused. Sadly, in our society today, there seems to be a constant mixed message being sent to our children. Lawson, in *Give to Live*, says that on the one hand we encourage our children to make money, be the best and win it all. On the other hand, we expect them to have a sense of responsibility to others and a compassionate and sharing heart. That makes it difficult for a child to determine which is more important. Perhaps the best way to teach children to care is to show them that caring for others will make them happy too. Caring is a win-win situation.

BE WILLING TO BEAR SOMEONE'S BURDEN

When we look at Christ's example we find clues for nurturing compassion. After His cousin John baptized Him, Jesus went into the wilderness, where He fasted for forty days and forty nights. Here at the beginning of His public ministry, He discovers what it feels like to be without food, without protection, without power, so that, in the future, He will understand those feelings when He encounters others in similar circumstances. Putting ourselves in the place of others and suffering with them can help us to be less judgmental, less self-righteous and less impatient of their failings.

This is called "projected feelings." In other words, we project how we think we would feel in a certain situation on to the person we are caring for. Actors use this technique to go deep into their emotions in order to project real feelings consistent with the role they are playing. For example, if an actor is to portray someone who has lost a parent, he or she will either relive a similar situation from personal experience or that of a close friend whom they observed. Projecting feelings is one way of finding compassion for others.

I remember years ago a friend of mine lost her first child at three days old. My friend was so deeply overwhelmed that I would have done anything to ease her pain—even if only for a moment. I prayed the prayer of intercession hoping that God would allow me to carry her burden temporarily. As I sat praying, I was overcome. Soon I was sobbing and felt as if my heart would break. Even now, as I write this, it brings me to tears.

Mark 14:33–35 (KJV) says that Jesus "began to be sore amazed, and to be very heavy; And saith unto them [his disciples], My soul is exceeding sorrowful. . . . And he went forward a little, and fell on the ground, and prayed. . . ." That is how I felt. I may not have relieved my friend's heartache, but I was certainly more able to empathize with her pain—and that helped me to better care for her.

The earlier in childhood that we learn to be caring, the more likely we are to develop altruistic (showing unselfish regard for others) personalities for life. But it is never too late to learn how to share the load of someone else's burden. By following Christ's example, we can all learn to be more caring.

SIMPLICITY MADE SIMPLE

Nurture compassion. Author Edith Wharton (1862–1937) said, "There are two ways of spreading light: to be the candle or the mirror that reflects it." Being compassionate is not just about noticing how others feel. It's about what we do when we see someone in pain. Offering compassion is an act that requires us to **SEE BEYOND OUR OWN NEEDS** and open our hearts to another.

There was an interesting study done that attempted to measure the healing effects of compassionate and loving intentions on breast cancer patients. It was called "The Love Study." One goal was to see if, with minimal training, people are capable of learning to **USE COMPASSIONATE INTENTION TO MAKE A DIFFERENCE** in their own lives, in the lives of their partners, in their relationships and in the course of their partner's illness. Although the conclusions are still unknown, the goal to better understand how such capacities can be nurtured brings hope for developing new approaches to improve the care for those suffering from a range of illnesses.[4]

USE YOUR DISAPPOINTMENTS TO DEVELOP COMPASSION. Everyone's life has its share of disappointments. Despite the fact that compassion and selflessness develop very early in life, many people shut down when faced with personal adversity. Our willingness to participate in the lives of others over our lifetime can exert a powerful influence on our adult patterns. Difficult experiences in life can make us better rather than bitter—it's simply a matter of conviction and determination to choose to be better.

FIND YOUR MOTIVATION FOR LEARNING TO CARE. Most of us are influenced by our early religious and spiritual training, by our family's examples and by traditions or cultural beliefs regarding our attitude to care. At any given time, the dominating motive for caring may differ depending on the circumstances. Simply caring because we believe it to be right should be enough motivation. But God knows we are weak so He gave us the added motivation of benefiting ourselves when we care. This is so strong and positive that once we experience the good (praise, recognition and appreciation) that comes from caring, it becomes a motive that we can adopt for living a life of caring. In their book *Life Is Uncertain . . . Eat Dessert First!*, Sol Gordon and Harold Brecher divide this response into three parts. First, we respond well to good feelings. Second, we try to experience good feelings again and again, being drawn to things that provide us consistent pleasure. Third, we become bored or dissatisfied with things that do not bring some kind of material or emotional reward. God knew that we would need praise, recognition and appreciation so He built these rewards into the care circle.

Lord, Your Word says, "Share each other's troubles and problems" (Galatians 6:2, NLT). I surrender my heart to You and am willing to let it break so that You can put it back together in the image of Your own. Empower me with love that brings healing to others in pain. Amen.

Teaching Children to Care

When Jesus saw this, he was indignant. He said to them,
"Let the little children come to me, and do not hinder them,
for the kingdom of God belongs to such as these."

—MARK 10:14 (NIV)

What a powerful experience it must have been for the children who sat at the feet of the Lord, to be cared for by the most caring of all—Jesus. His example shows us how simple it can be to teach children to care for others. All that children need in order to be caring and feel secure is a loving look and a gentle touch from someone who cares. They don't need to understand the process of caring intellectually in order to respond emotionally. Children believe us if they trust us. If they trust us, they can learn from us. The parents' example is especially important in determining whether or not a child becomes someone who cares and shares easily. The way parents and other close relatives behave and treat others is what a child will learn. Becoming a caring person is a lifelong process that evolves slowly and requires being exposed to many positive experiences.

There are daily opportunities for parents to assist their children in acquiring the necessary attitudes and life skills needed to develop caring instincts. I remember eating lunch with friends many years ago. We were in a family-style restaurant where large platters of food are served for all to share. One of the children, who was about seven years old at the time, proceeded to selectively take all the meat from the stew for herself, leaving only vegetables for the rest of us. This was a perfect opportunity for her mother to teach her how to share and be considerate of others. I waited hopefully for this to happen. But it didn't. That was sad, because it was even more important for this child because her early experiences were in an orphanage—what she learned there was to be greedy and Mom was missing a unique opportunity to teach her otherwise. Today, this now-grown young woman still struggles to feel empathy and be caring toward others. She finds it difficult to have compassion for relatives and other people, even for those she knows well.

Children's first efforts to care need to be encouraged. Their sense of social competence and pride must be enhanced. That way their natural capacity for kindness, coupled with repeated reinforcement of positive experiences, will be built on a solid foundation of caring skills. The young woman above is willing to learn—she simply needs to be taught cooperation, fairness and responsibility. She recently learned to express appreciation when someone does something nice for her rather than take it for granted. My husband and I had taken her to dinner several times and she never thanked us for it. Realizing that it never occurred to her to be thankful, I discussed it with her the next time I saw her. Last night after dinner, she made sure we knew she was grateful. Lesson simply learned!

CREATE OPPORTUNITIES FOR CHILDREN TO CARE FOR OTHERS

The friendships that children make also greatly influence their ability to care for others. It is in preschoolers' first friendships that they hone their ability to distinguish right from wrong and what is and isn't appropriate behavior. Of course, the process is helped when they have adults in their lives who are consistent, set fair limits and have realistic expectations based on their age. Sometimes parents make the mistake of assuming that kids think like adults— and they don't. Perceptions vary with age and so will their caring behavior. Even though a three-year-old is able to help a brother or sister with a task, it will be very different than the way an eight-year-old would help. It is also reasonable to expect an eight-year-old to share while a three-year-old may need you to be more patient.

In general, a two-year-old may try to comfort a crying playmate by offering a "blankie." She is not able to understand why her friend is crying, but she remembers times when she felt sad and Mommy gave her a blanket. At three, children are more aware of others. However, they still have trouble relating to how others actually feel. For example, they may delight in knocking down another's stack of blocks but not understand why that makes their playmate upset. By age four, they begin to understand when they've hurt someone and may even offer an apology without being told to do so. At age five or six, they share more easily and are willing to take turns. You can also engage them in discussions about what it means to be kind and help them to think of ways they can demonstrate kindness to others.

As children mature, their awareness of the world expands from themselves to their family, school, friends and community. It is only then that they can become concerned about social issues like homelessness. As they are learning to postpone personal gratification they also learn to tolerate some frustration in a healthy way. They learn these lessons in their day-to-day struggles as they come to terms with accepting a world that exists outside themselves. Caring children can be taught to help others and contribute to causes they feel passionate about if adults assist them in channeling their energy and providing positive reinforcement for their efforts. The best way to teach children empathy is to demonstrate it yourself, just as Christ did. Children who feel loved will find it easier to care about and empathize with others.

Guideposts writer Marion Bond West wrote about a dramatic demonstration of how children can learn to be compassionate and caring:

> Dorothy Miller had been a nun. She gave it up to become a mother. Never married, she adopted ten severely retarded, brain-damaged, emotionally disturbed children. Doctors insisted one underweight girl would only be a vegetable. Dorothy proved them wrong. There were spina bifida children, Down's syndrome and other diagnoses I didn't even begin to understand.
>
> Dorothy ran a tight ship. There was firm discipline, along with unrestrained love. No pity was allowed. Dorothy taught the children to help one another. It was amazing to watch their feeding, tooth-brushing and getting-into-leg-braces routine.
>
> One Sunday, after I was newly widowed, my teenage sons and I were having a heated argument while eating in a restaurant. I ended up crying, leaving my food untouched. Just then Dorothy and her brood came in—smiling, laughing, limping, some pushing wheelchairs. She saw me and waved, and they

got seated. One of her boys kept watching me. Finally, he came over, patted my shoulder, looked me directly in the eyes and said with slight speech impediment and a perfect smile, "I tan see ooh having a hard time. It will det better."

"Thank you," I responded, greatly encouraged, half laughing, half crying. He was right. It did get better. I still marvel over the compassion Dorothy Miller instills in each of her remarkable children. It's something I can learn—and be reminded of—from them.

SIMPLICITY MADE SIMPLE

Simply believe. Just as Christ did—believe that your children are capable of being kind. Children will meet the expectations you have for them. If you treat your children as if they are always up to no good, eventually they will meet your expectations and be up to no good. But if you **ASSUME THE BEST**, they will do their best to measure up.

MODEL POSITIVE ACTION. What you do says volumes. Rather than criticizing your children, let them catch you in the act of kindness. Simple role-modeling is the most effective way to teach.

TREAT CHILDREN WITH RESPECT. My friend Jan raised four boys and now teaches first graders. It never ceases to amaze me how a simple matter of attitude can make such a difference. Rather than demanding that children suddenly stop playing and leave the playground because it's time to go, she alerts them when playtime is *almost* over. That way, they know what is expected and have time to prepare to leave.

ACKNOWLEDGE KINDNESS. Don't ever miss an opportunity to encourage a child to be more caring by noticing when she or he demonstrates a caring attitude. Also, be sure to point out others' demonstrations of kindness. For example, if someone treats you well, be sure to acknowledge their efforts and praise them in front of your child.

Be patient. **PATIENCE BEGETS PATIENCE.** Kindness and compassion are the bedrock of patience. Being a loving and tolerant person will help you raise wonderful and caring children.

BE HONEST. Tell your children how you feel when they say or do something that upsets you. Words have power. Let your children know the consequences of their words and how they can hurt or heal.

Don't teach rudeness. **DON'T LET RUDENESS PASS.** If someone is rude to you, acknowledge it, but also explain that perhaps that person was simply having a bad day. This helps to teach children that when someone is nasty to you, you don't have to be nasty in return. If your child is rude to you, do as my friend Jan does with her brood and ask, "Would you like to try that again?" They almost always change their attitude and get it right with that second try.

> Lord, I am grateful for a new chance at being a caring person. Each day You give me fresh opportunities to demonstrate kindness toward someone. Today I will pass the test. I will remember that You have hidden happiness in serving others rather than in being served myself. Amen.

Teaching an Old Dog
New Tricks

"I loathe my very life; therefore I will give free rein to my
complaint and speak out in the bitterness of my soul."

—JOB 10:1 (NIV)

When we are up against life and it seems full of affliction, it is easy to feel sorry for ourselves. Our pain can tempt us toward self-pity. Unfortunately, self-pity can lead to self-righteousness. And that can cause us to become one of those people who keeps track of all of life's injustices. Soon, we sound like Job complaining that life is unfair. We may even begin to question God's motives—blaming Him for our condition. What we need to do instead is remember that life's trials can be the means for our development and refinement. Instead of feeling sorry for ourselves, looking for revenge and wallowing in self-pity, we should ask, "What can I learn and how can I grow through this experience?"

Inside each of us is a persistent voice. Some call this "self-talk." It is what we tell ourselves as we experience life. For some of us it is an encouraging voice.

But, unfortunately, for others it is the voice of discontent. A discontented inner voice is constantly critical of life, the world and almost everything we say and do. As children, we learned to listen to this voice and to believe what it said. If the voice you have been living with is cruel, punishing and full of self-hate, then you may have a hard time being kind and caring toward others because you have a hard time being kind toward yourself. If your inner voice has continually told you that you will never measure up, then you probably suffer from lack of confidence that hinders your ability to reach out to others. The good news is that none of the negative stuff you've been telling yourself was ever true. You simply have to learn to have compassion for yourself and be willing to forgive those who have hurt you.

CARE ENOUGH TO LET GO OF UNFORGIVENESS

Matthew 6:14–15 says if you forgive others for the wrongs they do to you, your Father in heaven will forgive you. But if you don't forgive others, your Father will not forgive your sins. Forgiveness is the critical element in the healing and releasing of past resentments. David Augsburger, professor of pastoral care at Fuller Theological Seminary and author of *Freedom of Forgiveness*, writes, "Forgiveness is letting what was, be gone, what will be, come, what is now, be. In *forgiving*, I finish my demands on past difficulties, problems, failures and say good-by to them with determination. I *cancel* my predictions, and suspicions of future failure, and welcome the next moment *with openness* to discover what will be."

In many ways, the concept of forgiveness is as simple as salvation—when we are saved, we are made new. Christ's forgiveness allows us to let go of the past and all the hurts involved and adopt a new attitude that has a positive outlook for the future. When we are finally able to care enough to forgive ourselves, release the past and accept the future realizing that God loves us, forgives us, and accepts us, then we will be able to reach out and care for others.

It's comforting to know, as we work through this process, that whole, unbruised and unbroken people are of little use to God. It is only when we have learned *agape* love through the circumstances of life that mold us and make us pliable that we can truly be of use to God in caring for others.

I love the way Guideposts writer Fay Angus expressed her own lesson of letting go:

> The half-mile narrow trail around Lake George in the high Sierra to our favorite fishing hole is beautiful but treacherous. Laden down with fishing gear and haversacks, my husband and I walked carefully beside flaming red fireweed and gold California poppies, digging our heels into the crumbly shale to keep from sliding down the steep bank.
>
> "Hold on to a branch to steady yourself as you come down!" John called up as he waited for me at the water's edge. Stepping down from a large rock, I grabbed for a branch and was gingerly groping for a foothold when I slipped. Suddenly, I was falling, and with an ominous snap the branch I was holding onto broke. I skidded down the rocky bank and would have plummeted into the lake had John not been there to catch me.
>
> "Are you hurt, honey?"
>
> Yes, I was hurt.
>
> I limped painfully back to our van for the bumpy ride to the local hospital. X-rays showed that I had cracked my tailbone, not seriously, but enough to cause discomfort for several weeks.

"For heaven's sake, lovey," John said, "you should have known better than to hold on to deadwood."

Unable to fish with John for the remainder of our vacation, I had lots of time to think about what he had said. I discovered that I had held onto deadwood not only by the lake, but in the rest of my life too. The "if only I had" of regrets and guilt. Resentment. A grudge held onto for years and years. "Lord," I prayed, "help me to let go of the deadwood in my heart."

Now I've learned to reach for living branches that will not let me down. On the lakeside trail, they're branches growing green. In my heart, they're faith and forgiveness.

S I M P L I C I T Y   M A D E   S I M P L E

Get rid of the deadwood in your life. No matter how old you are, you are still capable of **LEARNING TO LET GO** and care. It's simply a matter of being willing. Sometimes, we must first accept emotionally as well as realistically the painful experiences before we can truly let go. But that can be a painful experience in and of itself. As we grieve and regrieve, we more fully absorb the whole impact. And that can temporarily create more pain. Augsburger put it this way, "The heart has a memory too, and it must be allowed to feel its pain *fully* before *releasing its hold on the past*."

STOP BEING SUSPICIOUS. Suspicion is a fearful attempt to hold back future pain. In suspecting the worst of everyone and everything, we force ourselves to put up emotional walls for self-protection. In doing so, we also eliminate the possibility of true intimacy and love because we are afraid to risk the possibility of someone hurting us again.

CULTIVATE A HEART FILLED WITH COMPASSION. Matthew Fox, author of *A Spirituality Named Compassion,* says, "The difference between persons and groups of persons is not that some are victims and some are not: we are all victims and all dying from lack of compassion; we are all surrendering our humanity together. The difference is in how persons react to this fact of compassion's exile and our victimization." When we follow Christ's teaching we recognize that His purpose was to model a way of life that is compassionate.

WE ARE ALL CONNECTED, so drive with love. I read a story about a gal who used her time driving home through traffic as a classroom for cultivating compassion. As she drove she repeated, "Drive with love, drive with love, drive with love." She decided that traffic was her test. But despite her driving with love, she was involved in a traffic accident. She was the first one struck in what turned out to be a four-car pileup. She said, "It was our 'connectedness that struck me.' Even though I was 'driving with love'—trying to be compassionate to the people around me—just one person who believes we are completely separate from each other, cut off by class, race, sexual orientations, religious beliefs or any other barrier that humans create, can wreak havoc for all of us." To be truly compassionate, we must be willing to be vulnerable and fully open with our hearts and minds to the experiences of others. We cannot simply sit along the sidelines watching.

LEARN COMPASSION BY BEING INFORMED and looking for ways to actively care for others. You cannot help care for the world if you do not know what is going on in it. Read the newspaper and watch the television news. Then identify with those you have read about or watched. Remember that these people are mothers, brothers, daughters, sisters and grandparents—just like you. Once you are aware of the issues that threaten our security and livelihood, choose to act to alleviate suffering and rectify injustice by getting involved. You can participate on a political level or simply by helping to support a family in your area that needs assistance.

SEEK TO UNDERSTAND GOD'S HEART FOR PEOPLE. For example, try walking and praying. You can do this at school, work or even in your neighborhood. As you walk, observe people with a heart that is seeking to follow the will of God and ask Him to give you a heart of compassion. Study the Gospels. When you read, read with an eye to seeing the heart of Jesus. As you study Matthew, Mark, Luke and John, you will find yourself understanding more intimately Jesus' heart.

Lord, forgive me for the times I have wondered why You didn't do something about someone's pain, when all the time You were waiting for me to do something for the person who was hurting. Right now, in Your presence, I let go of the deadwood of unforgiveness that I have held against others, and I hold Your fresh, living Word to keep my feet from stumbling. Make me sure-footed so that I will be able to show others the path to Your blessings. Amen.

Caring Enough to Confront

For the sinful nature desires what is contrary
to the Spirit, and the Spirit what is contrary to the
sinful nature. They are in conflict with each other,
so that you do not do what you want.

—GALATIANS 5:17 (NIV)

The apostle Paul described two spiritual principles that are in deep and irreconcilable conflict. Our sinful nature does no good and does not desire good, whereas God's Holy Spirit does no evil and opposes anything that does not please God. As followers of our faith, our sinful nature is to become increasingly subdued as we learn of God's grace, which gives us the power to walk in ways of His Spirit. Yet the conflict between these two opposing desires will never be eliminated completely in this life. As a result, we will never be released from the necessity of consciously choosing to go in God's way and to depend on His grace to do what is right.

The same conflict is true in our patterns of responding to life's experiences and our behavior within our relationships. We are largely the products of our past and a consequence of our early childhood development. We have basically been conditioned by our social situations. The way we handle conflict is a pattern that we learned over a lifetime of experiences. The problem with this is that not all ways of handling conflict are healthy or beneficial to our current relationships. Some of us have learned to defeat others. Erroneously, we believe that when we have a conflict with someone, we are right, he is wrong, and there is no in-between. This is a demonstration of power with no room for love. Others may choose the flight response. They simply can't deal with conflict so they either ignore the situation or run from it—withdrawing from the problem. This leaves no room at all for resolving conflict. Some choose to just give in. This may make them appear to be nice people, but it can also make them secretly resentful. When a person feels dominated, he or she can become frustrated and that can eventually lead to a total collapse of the relationship. Compromise is another option. It sounds good and is often an effective way to help resolve conflicts. In fact, it can be a gift in the midst of serious conflict. But if conflict requires us to compromise on our foundational beliefs—the cost may be too high.

Augsburger, in *Caring Enough to Confront*, says, "When we begin with a decision to compromise, we run the risk that my half of the truth added to your half may not give us the whole truth and nothing but the truth. We may have two half-truths. Only when we care enough to tussle with the truth can we test, retest, refine and perhaps find more of it through our working at it seriously."

Caring enough to confront says that we want a relationship that allows us to be in a position of honesty and integrity. To accomplish this we must change our view of "conflict." We must realize that conflict is neither good nor bad—it is simply neutral and natural. As we learn to work through our differences by giving clear messages that say, "I care" and "I want," we will find the most helpful ways to care and confront.

Confrontation is an intimidating word. Many of us connect it with "bad" feelings. We get riled up, defensive and ready to shoot. But just because someone has a different opinion than we have doesn't mean she is rejecting us. Just because she disagrees with us doesn't mean she is attacking us. When we confront someone, we are simply inviting the opportunity for change. Change is what is necessary in order for us to grow. And growth is exactly what God has in mind for all of our lives. So why do we resist it? Because it's scary. Augsburger says, "Life without confrontation is directionless, aimless, passive. When unchallenged, human beings tend to drift, to wander or to stagnate."

DEVELOP THE ART OF CONFRONTATION

It's not the confronting that's the problem—it's how we do it that causes the problem. There is an art to confronting and it is something that can be learned. To be caustic, critical and sarcastic is not the way to confront. We must be clear, caring and candid. We must be able to offer the maximum amount of information about the other person's part in the relationship with a minimum amount of threat to the relationship. As we learn, step-by-step, we will establish new ways of responding to each other and the situations in which we find ourselves. But the caring must come first.

The people we are confronting must know without a doubt that we truly care for them, support and trust them. Augsburger writes, "Building a solidarity in relationships with others—through caring, support, empathy, trust, affirmation, understanding and love—provides a foundation for the more powerful actions of confrontation, criticism, evaluation, counsel, assertiveness, disagreement and open leveling with each other."

The foundation for confrontation is love. I read a Guideposts article by Ruth Evans titled "Runaway Mother" that illustrates the right and wrong way to confront. Ruth discovered a pile of beer and wine bottles under a tarp in the basement. Her daughter Joan had just turned seventeen. Up until that discovery, Ruth felt good about her family, believing that they had mutual consideration and that each of them respected each other's privacy, their home and that they were all following certain guidelines of behavior so as not to hurt one another.

Desperate to find the truth about the beer and wine bottles, she did something she never expected to do—she read her daughter's diary. The evidence was there. Ruth left the diary on Joan's bed, open to the incriminating page. Ruth felt betrayed. She felt her daughter had betrayed the entire family. But she also felt guilty about reading the diary, breaking their covenant of privacy. When her daughter realized the discovery, she too had mixed emotions of anger and shame. When she attempted to explain to her mother, Ruth found it impossible to listen. She couldn't see her daughter—instead she saw only a stranger that she could not believe. Ruth panicked and took off in the car leaving her daughter alone to deal with her emotions. She wrote:

> It began to get dark, so I pulled off the highway and stopped the car on the shoulder of a narrow country road. I laid my face against the steering wheel and closed my eyes. I hadn't really prayed for many years, yet there in the twilight the words came as effortlessly as when I was a child.
>
> I must have dozed, because when I raised my head it was

pitch black. I started the car and drove. At a crossroads was a small, white clapboard church. I stopped the car. I had to strain to read the name, dimly illuminated by a nearby street lamp. There was no one about, so I got out of the car to get a closer look. Hand-carved gilt letters above the doors spelled the words: The Church of the Covenant.

"Covenant." Joan's white and frightened face appeared before me. "Poor baby," I sighed. Then I understood. I knew what God wanted me to do. He had led me and comforted me. Surely I could do the same for my child . . . His child.

The next day we were able to confront each other, openly, across the dining-room table. Yes, she had let her friends come over. Then more who weren't her friends came and she didn't know how to stop them. No, she didn't drink. She'd tried it, but it made her feel awful. Yes, she had lied to me because she was afraid of upsetting me.

All that happened over a year ago. Joan and I have been able to rebuild our trust in each other. Soon Joan will be going to college.

What made the difference for this mother and daughter was the intervention of God through prayer.

SIMPLICITY MADE SIMPLE

Experience the freedom of change. Many of us are simply stuck in old ways of operating. We continue to respond to life as we learned to do as children.

But today's relationships involve different people. Today's experiences are different from the past. The past is gone—so too should be our old ways of responding. We need to **LEARN NEW AND DIFFERENT SKILLS** that are appropriate for our lives today. There are a lot of books that deal with relationship patterns, or try a Christian counseling service.

CONFRONTATION IS THE KEY to change. Nothing will happen, we won't grow and things won't get better unless we find ways of challenging the status quo. Even when we don't confront, think of how much energy it takes just to preserve things as they are.

Rehearse before confronting. **DO A MENTAL REHEARSAL** of both caring and confronting. Practice saying, "I do care, I want to respect you, I want your respect. But I want you to know how I feel. I want to better our relationship." Put yourself in the other's position and try to experience this situation as he or she will.

CONFRONT CARINGLY, GENTLY, CONSTRUCTIVELY, acceptingly and clearly.

Remember that **TRUST IS THE ROOT EMOTION**. In stress, it's easy to fall back into old ways. So trust must be reinforced. Trust is an attitude that can be inferred from our actions and our words. We should not be constantly evaluating others or their personalities. We must be careful in how we make judgmental statements, being sure they are directed toward "behavior" and not the "behaver." We must respect the feelings of the other and not attempt to control someone else's words or expressions of feelings. All feeling needs to be validated. We must not attempt to manipulate or threaten. Make simple, honest statements and clear, open requests. Be willing to be vulnerable.

Pray. **REMEMBER THAT GOD IS AMONG US**. He has our best interest at heart. He is willing to intervene and guide us. You just have to ask.

Lord, help me to remember that my honest feelings may
not be the same as Your truth. Help me seek the truth when
I feel conflict with those who are in my care. Give me
understanding to see more sides than my own viewpoint,
and keep us all bound together with Your love. Amen.

Sympathy vs. Empathy

Their insults have broken my heart, and I am in despair.

If only one person would show some pity;

if only one would turn and comfort me.

—PSALM 69:20 (NLT)

David, the writer of Psalms, was looking for someone who could identify with his feelings, have sympathy and offer comfort, but instead those around him were indeed enemies, not friends. They did their best to make things worse for him. Finally, David quieted himself as he realized that God knew everything about him—including his scorn, disgrace and shame—but God still loved him.

That's what makes life unique for those who believe—we have Someone who always knows exactly how and what we feel and is willing to take action on our behalf. For us, only mere humans, such ability does not necessarily come naturally. Why? Because there is a process through which we must advance and mature until we are ultimately led to a place of empathy that can result in moving us to action. It is the sum of our life experiences that helps to move us along this pathway.

The process often starts with pity. Pity is simply concern brought on by the misfortune or suffering of others. As pity deepens, some of us will feel a sense of suffering with the pitiable. This is sympathy. Sympathy denotes the capacity for sharing in the sorrows or troubles of another. That's part of what David was looking for—but he still needed more. He needed empathy, which is a deep awareness of the suffering of another *and* the desire to relieve it. You can have pity and be sympathetic toward someone—but that does not make you empathetic.

EMPATHY IS LOVE IN ACTION

You cannot, however, have empathy without pity and sympathy. For example, you may take pity and feel bad when you see a blind person on the street struggling to find his way, but you simply walk on by. Some of us may even be able to reach the point of feeling sympathy—but that is not enough. There is a big difference between *sympathy* and *empathy*. The empathetic person would offer to help the blind person. It is this degree of empathetic understanding and ability to feel compassion that enables us to care effectively for the suffering.

I was working at an interior design firm where one of the designers got stuck in the sympathy phase of caring for her clients. She wanted to give them the best for the least. The problem this caused is that in reality you cannot have the best for the least. And that led to frustration for everyone. Her desire to solve all the clients' problems and give them an amazingly beautiful room required budgets larger than her clients had. If she could have moved to the next level, which is empathy, she would have instead been able to search for creative ways to solve problems for less, and help her clients compromise where necessary.

Sometimes having empathy creates a dilemma: "Is it more caring to help or to let the other person work through her problem on her own?" It may be more beneficial to let someone learn through making some mistakes rather than simply extending a helping hand. On the level of appearance, this may look like we don't care despite the reality that we indeed do care and simply made the decision that would be the best for the person involved. This is a common dilemma, especially when raising children. In fact, letting a child struggle through a challenge may very likely "hurt us more than it hurts the child."

The difference between sympathy and empathy was well illustrated in the following story by Ellen Secrest written for Guideposts:

> I jumped out of the car and ran up the front steps of the old apartment house. It was my turn to deliver a hot meal to the elderly woman in Apartment 23-C. She was very sweet, very lonely and loved to chat, but I never gave her a chance to say anything.
>
> You see, this woman was fond of cats and shared her tiny apartment with six adored felines. The problem was litter boxes. There just weren't enough of them to handle this household. So each time I stepped inside her door, I smiled, put the lunch tray down on the nearest table and made a rapid retreat—holding my breath until I got back into the hall.
>
> Then one day, I heard a story about an old rabbi who asked his students how they knew when nighttime had ended and the new day had begun. One pupil thought it happened when one saw an animal in the distance and was able to tell whether it

was a sheep or a dog. Another guessed that it happened when one looked at a tree in the distance and could tell whether it was a fig tree or a peach tree. The wise rabbi shook his head at both of these answers.

"Then how can you tell when night has ended?" the students asked.

"You can tell when you look at a face of any human being and see that he is your brother or sister. If you cannot do this, then it is still night."

The next time I visited the old woman's apartment I lingered for a little while. Her smile and the light that came into her eyes made the place bearable. Shortly after, a group of us contacted a local social services agency, explained the situation and made arrangements for weekly housecleaning to be done. Now she is living with the cats she loves in a healthy environment— and I'm taking the time to get to know her better.

It's amazing what can happen when we finally make the transitions from pity to sympathy to empathy. Our goal should be to progress to yet the next level of caring—*altruism*. Altruism is related to pity, sympathy and empathy. It is unselfish concern for the welfare of others that is characterized by charitable acts.

SIMPLICITY MADE SIMPLE

Empathy is action. **EMPATHETIC FEELINGS LEAD TO EMPATHETIC ACTIONS.** Even if those actions are the decision to let the person work through her problem for her own benefit. This is different from simply watching her struggle and not caring how she feels. Empathy is processing the emotions and understanding the facts of the situation and coming to a conclusion that takes the interest of the other to heart.

EXPERIENCE EMPATHY AND DO GOOD. Unfortunately, empathy doesn't always lead to good deeds. The good side of empathy is a genuine and authentic concern for another. The evil side of empathy uses the knowledge and understanding that has been gained to *play* at empathy. One gains the trust of the other and then manipulates him. That's because empathy depends not only on one's ability to identify with someone else's emotions but also on one's capacity to put oneself in the other person's place and to experience an appropriate emotional response.

BE VULNERABLE. Only when we are vulnerable are we able to experience the full range of emotions in the world around us. Vulnerability is the unique capability that allows us to acknowledge and care for others responsibly.

Accept the fact that **SOMETIMES YOU CANNOT HELP** even if you do care. Just because you have processed through all the phases and feel as if you are walking in someone's shoes, it still does not obligate you to making the person change. She may by choice have chosen to wear a pair of high-heeled sneakers that are two sizes too small. That is her choice—and there is nothing you can do to relieve the pain in her feet unless she decides she is ready for change.

LIFE EXPERIENCES CAN HELP OR HINDER our ability to have empathy. Sometimes people who have endured great pains are less able to identify with situations that are relatively trivial compared with lives of tremendous suffering. It's a matter of perspective. The ruler against which they measure things as worthy of upset can be fairly rigid. Others may have built a protective wall around themselves to keep from being hurt again. That wall now makes it impossible for them to feel anyone else's pain as well.

Father, the more I care for others the less I worry about myself. You have created us for good works, and I pray that I will find ways to give more of my time and talents to others so there is more room for You to shine through me each day. Amen.

Caring Connects Us with God's Plan

GOD NEVER INTENDED for any of us to feel uncared for or alone. We are all connected to each other in some way. He wants us to care for each other, and when we give care God's way, He revitalizes us and keeps us from "burning out." In Part Three, I will share ways to find a balance in caring for yourself, your spouse, your children, your neighbors and God's creation. Following God's leading will keep you from feeling burdened by giving attention to so many different concerns. And as our children see the way we care for them and for what God has given to us, they will learn to help us tend and keep what we have been entrusted with. God has hidden heroes all around us who deserve to be affirmed and appreciated. After reading the next section, simply ask God to reveal new ways to show you how to care for those He has placed in your life.

Caring for Yourself

Timothy, guard what has been entrusted to your care.

Turn away from godless chatter and the opposing ideas

of what is falsely called knowledge.

—1 TIMOTHY 6:20 (NIV)

At the close of Paul's letter to Timothy, he summarizes his instruction: "Guard what has been entrusted to your care." Timothy was to turn away from what other teachers were saying, such as the doctrine taught by Gnostics—those who professed to a superior knowledge and believed that salvation came only to those who had their secret.

Hmm . . . those false teachers sound a lot like today's advertising messages: "Start losing weight in less than seventy-two hours, and notice results by next weekend—we've got the secret!" Another intriguing ad reads: "Why a Right Hand Ring? You've Earned It!"

Yes, Paul was talking about guarding our faith, but guarding our faith requires that we also guard against the daily temptations that society has come to believe are important and even necessary for life. That means we must learn to disseminate the information we are bombarded with every day and determine what is and is not important in caring for ourselves physically and spiritually.

Recently, a friend of mine had breast enlargement surgery. She had been talking about it for years, and finally made the decision to go ahead and do it. The surgery and recovery have been much more painful than she imagined. She now hopes that this has all been worth it. So why did she ultimately choose to have this surgery? Because she has suffered her whole life with low self-esteem and never really considered herself *worthy* of true love. If she simply accepted God's love for her, she would know that He considers her very worthy of love because He already loves her. But accepting ourselves enough to love ourselves can be difficult. And unless we do, we will not be very good at caring for ourselves or anyone else.

DESTRESS YOUR LIFE

Accepting ourselves allows us to be in the presence of others honestly. True friendships result from our individual ability to unconditionally accept and love each other. Our acceptance of others and their unique differences is directly related to our ability to accept ourselves.

Loving ourselves and others requires "Sonlight" and nourishment. The only way we can obtain such light and nourishment is to be willing to receive it directly from the source of love itself. That means opening our hearts to God's truth with discernment. Filling ourselves with knowledge of God's

Word will allow us to still protect ourselves and guard against false teachers while obtaining what we need for body and soul. It's simply about finding the right balance.

Living a balanced life is key to caring for yourself. This means establishing the highest level of integrity possible but not beating yourself up when you fail. Karen Mains, author of *Comforting One Another*, says, "I am not nearly as important as I think I am, but I am much more important than I know." This is the paradox that trips us up. All of us struggle daily with finding the balance between our importance and the lack thereof. Just because we don't feel worthy or important today does not mean God's view of us has changed. He still loves us and forgives us and wants us to know the truth of His love for us. He desires the best for us. Therefore, we should settle for no less in caring for ourselves.

Joyce Good Reis wrote in an inspiring and practical article for Guideposts about her struggle to find balance in her life:

> I was ready to quit my job as an operating nurse. I was frustrated, and felt as though I wasn't giving my all.
>
> At home, the children seemed to be bickering more than usual, we never managed to sit down together for dinner, and whenever I tried to find time for prayer or Bible study, my attention wandered. Frantically, I sought answers: a new position in my department, a new church, a psychologist to help me communicate with my oldest son. But the more I chased after help, the more run down I became. What was wrong? To put it simply, I was burned out.
>
> Psychologists say burnout is the depletion of caring

energies following the accumulation of chronic stress. It often occurs when we confront daily situations we cannot change.

But this downward progression can be stopped. From my nursing experience, I knew about the importance of rest, diet and exercise in stress management. But I needed to do more to rekindle my spirits. In time I learned there were things I could do.

1. *Narrow the focus of your life*. Learn to say no. Set short-term goals and prioritize to eliminate some of the pressures in your life. Accepting the fact that you cannot be all things to all persons is a vital first step toward cutting stress. For me, it meant giving up leading a fellowship group and not teaching a Sunday school class. I needed to become a listener for a time.

2. *Be specific in prayer*. This is not the time in your life to concentrate on prayers for world peace and an end to famine. Ask instead for the strength to make it through the next hour, then the next day. Keep prayers simple and specific. Sometimes when I'm having trouble praying, I just say the Lord's Prayer over and over again, slowly, thinking of the words. Keeping a prayer journal also helps me reflect on my real needs.

3. *Seek the support of friends*. I have a dear friend who, without my asking, took the children on an overnight camping trip to give me time to myself. Another friend has made it clear I can call her anytime, day or night, if I need someone to talk to. Friendships like these counter the sense of isolation, provide distraction and boost my sagging self-esteem.

4. *Be patient.* Learn to wait on God's timing. Give your burdens to Him, then live by His calendar. Schedule time for yourself—for playing, resting, reading, praying, nurturing, encouraging and listening. Slow down your pace and give Him the opportunity to work in your life.

I remember a child's joke that goes, "How do you eat an elephant? One bite at a time." Burnout does not occur overnight, and neither does its cure. Many things help, but most important is learning to take smaller bites every day.

Remember also that to be burned out, you must first have been on fire! The fire and zeal of the spirit can be rekindled so that it will burn even brighter. Like any fire, it requires careful tending and refueling to burn on without consuming itself.

SIMPLICITY MADE SIMPLE

Express yourself. You must be willing to express your feelings. The best way to get your needs met is simply to **ASK FOR WHAT YOU WANT**. This means you must learn to express your feelings instead of repressing them.

Take time to play. Just as we encourage children to get outside and **GET SOME FRESH AIR**, we should do the same. Connecting with nature is exhilarating and rejuvenating to our bodies and our souls. Take time to explore the freedom of God's blessings in His creation outside. Listen for the singing of birds, the trickling of water or even the sound of wind as it rustles through the trees. Then quiet yourself and listen for the voice of your Creator.

Be grateful. Find at least one thing every day to be grateful for. Then rejoice in the good fortune of that gift. **CHOOSE HAPPINESS**. Make choices that bring you more happiness by selecting things that bring you love and laughter. Spend a few minutes each day doing one thing that makes you feel peaceful such as burning a candle, enjoying a cup of tea or reading a good book.

Celebrate your life by **CARING FOR YOUR BODY, MIND AND SOUL**. Set aside time in your calendar to exercise, learn something new and listen to your dreams. Sign up for a class that you've been thinking about. My friend Jan encouraged me to try a Pilates Reformer class—and six months later I am thrilled with the positive results it has brought to my life. Not only have I become stronger and reduced my body fat, but I have made new friends too!

Pray. There is nothing more renewing than getting nourishment from the Source. Set your alarm early to **CREATE TIME FOR PRAYER AND MEDITATION**. Start with a Bible verse. Take time to reflect, then organize your day as God directs.

> **Lord, You said that if I follow You my burden would be light, but I have the tendency to pick up cares and concerns that You never asked me to carry. I ask for discernment to know what cares are from You and what burdens I am to lay at Your feet. Create in me a clean heart and rekindle my zeal for the abundant life You have provided for me. Amen.**

Caring for Children

Before I got married I had six theories about bringing up children; now I have six children, and no theories.

—JOHN WILMOT, SECOND EARL OF ROCHESTER (1647–1680)

This quote simply proves that the more things change, the more they remain the same. Raising and caring for children has never been easy. Charles L. Rassieur, counselor pastor and author of the book *Christian Renewal*, said, "Indeed, I have discovered that the more I try to control my children, the more resistant they become to my advice and parental wisdom." What makes this interesting is that eventually this statement will reverse itself and reflect a child's dilemma about his or her parents. "Just as parents must learn the spiritual truth that they cannot control their children's well-being, even so must children often learn, in their later years, that they cannot control their aging parents."

God has made each of us a unique individual, and that presents a challenge when attempting to develop a simple "how-to" on caring for children. Each child has a special way of responding to his or her environment. As the eldest of six children, I never cease to be amazed at how differently we each turned out.

Children clearly need love—and lots of it—but they also need understanding. Without an understanding of your children's needs, you cannot effectively support them.

Author of *Children Are from Heaven*, John Gray, says, "Nurturing and not breaking a child's will is the basis of creating confidence, cooperation, and compassion in children." If we want children to grow up to live lives that model Christ's example, then we must nurture compassion by caring for them in ways they are most able to receive it.

Gray suggests there are four different temperaments that children fall into: sensitive children, active children, responsive children and receptive children. *Sensitive* children are more vulnerable, dramatic and more feeling than other children. They have a greater need to identify what they are feeling and once they have, they are more willing to make a change. They respond best to those who listen and take the time to understand them. Because sensitive children learn about themselves by identifying their wants and sharing their feelings, they complain a lot. It's simply part of their nature and the way they process information about themselves. The good news is that when you give them an opportunity to share their burdens, they lighten up. They don't need you to cheer them up—they need you to validate and have empathy toward their feelings. They also need to know that they are not the only ones feeling this way. They need to know that they are not the only ones who suffer.

Active children, as the name implies, are more interested in *doing* than in exploring their inner responses to life. Active children need preparation and structure, otherwise they easily get out of control and become resistant to authority. They need to know in advance what the game plan is. Active children also thrive in leadership positions as long as they are given clear guidelines for operating. They have lots of energy and simply cannot be expected to sit still for very long. They learn best from their own mistakes, but they also need lots of grace and forgiveness when they make them. They benefit much when their successes are acknowledged. When they are cared for this way, they become cooperative and supportive individuals.

Responsive children are social butterflies. They are outgoing and develop their sense of self from their responses to the world and their relationships. They are self-motivated and want to experience everything life has to offer. Each new experience brings out another aspect of their personality and talent. That's good—but it's also bad because responsive children have a hard time staying focused. Just like the butterfly, they like to flit from one flower to another. They are simply too easily distracted. They need a lot of direction about what to do to stay on task. Their temperament also makes them forgetful. It is not unusual for responsive children to completely forget your instructions. It's not a matter of disobedience or defiance—they just forgot what you said. As they grow, they will gradually learn how to stay focused. In the meantime, don't expect these children to create order in their lives or keep a tidy room, unless you are willing to help them. Caring for responsive children requires the giving of support to keep them from becoming overwhelmed. When you care for them this way, you will be rewarded with solid, responsible, self-directed and confident adults.

The fourth temperament is the *receptive* child. Receptive children need to have a "flow" to their life. They want to know what the day will bring, what to expect. My goddaughter is receptive. The problem is that her mother is responsive. And those two mix as badly as oil and water. If you put receptive children in a situation where they don't know what to expect, then you can expect resistance. They learn to know themselves by knowing what they expect to happen. Their lives must be structured with routines, repetition and specific times for eating, sleeping and even playing. Receptive children need time to come to their own conclusions and more time to do things in an orderly fashion, and they are not good at accepting change quickly. They need to think things over. To help receptive children develop into all that they can be means that you must be willing to help them by giving them tasks. For example, without your help they may never develop any outside interests because they are quite content to simply sit and observe others.

ADAPT TO YOUR CHILD'S NEEDS

As much as my goddaughter wanted to learn to sing, she could never bring herself to take lessons. I offered to pay for classes and even to go with her if she wanted, to no avail. Receptive children need the security of a regular routine to give them the support and confidence necessary to take the risk to try something new. Most importantly, receptive children need rituals for love. Loving rituals help these children by giving them a venue for experiencing their worthiness in a special connection with each parent. With my goddaughter, I would simply sing the same lullaby (out of tune) to her every time she spent the night at my house. Later, lunch at the same restaurant became her love ritual with me.

The temperaments are good guidelines for how to care for our children—but recognize that most children are a combination of more than just one temperament. Also remember that you can't always give your children what they want—and that's okay as long as you are giving them what they need. Even the simple act of listening to a child's feelings will give a child what he or she needs.

Carol Kuykendall wrote about an experience with her daughter for Guideposts that illustrates the rewards of caring for children:

> Our whole family sat together in a circle on a blanket, munching fried chicken at the end-of-the-season Teen Tennis picnic one August evening. Correction! Four and a half members of our family sat together. Lindsay, fourteen, was only half there, which is the way she had seemed most of the time lately. She perched on the edge of the blanket, her back to us, laughing with her friends. I missed her constant chatter and little-girl grin in our family circle. I started feeling sorry for myself and my sad turned to mad. *Insensitive, inconsiderate, uncaring* were some of the "mad" words buzzing through my head as the tennis coaches began announcing the annual awards.
>
> First was Most Improved, then Most Valuable; next was Sportsmanship. "This award goes to the person who knows the importance of being a team player. She's always a good sport, no matter how many changes we make. She's consistently the most *sensitive, considerate, caring* member of our team. Lindsay Kuykendall!"
>
> Lindsay turned around, flashed us her little-girl grin and marched up to claim her trophy. I sat in stunned silence for a moment, and then started clapping loudly. Not only for her, but for the lesson I'd just learned about the importance of being a team player and a good sport on our family team— especially as our circle gently changes shape.

The best way to care for children is simply prepare them to leave the nest.

SIMPLICITY MADE SIMPLE

LEARN TO COMMUNICATE. Gail and Gordon MacDonald, in their book *If Those Who Reach Could Touch*, say, "Perhaps the simplest and the most difficult thing for many people to do in friendships, family relationships or marriages is to talk—talk in such a way that there is a satisfying exchange that leaves everyone in a state of fulfillment and wholeness." Christ loved His disciples simply by communicating with them. He told them stories. He answered their questions, and He gave directions for life.

Listen. **HALF OF COMMUNICATION IS LISTENING.** The more you listen, the more you will understand. The better you understand, the better you can care for those you love.

TOUCH YOUR CHILDREN. Research reveals that when premature infants are given short daily massages, their growth rate is increased by nearly fifty percent. Karen Mains, in *Comforting One Another*, notes that "a study at the Touch Institute discovered that when parents of diabetic children gave nightly massages, both the parents and the children had less anxiety and depression; in addition, the physiological effect also dramatically lowered the children's blood-glucose levels to normal range.... The deeper meaning of touching or holding is its potential sacramentally; touch has the power to convey something of God through a very human means. This is an essential message of the Incarnation. Christ took on flesh to make God knowable; we, filled with the Spirit of this Christ, can do the same."

Kids can learn empathy and compassion if they grow up caring for an animal. **PETS CAN NURTURE COMPASSION, EMPATHY AND RESPONSIBILITY** in children. In return, children receive love and devotion from a pet.

Lord, forgive me for selfish moments when I am convinced that I need something from the children You have put in my life, and help me to recognize what they need from me. I realize You have put them in my life so that I can influence them to choose what is good and pleasing to You. Bless the fleeting moments that we have together with warm examples of unconditional love. Amen.

Caring for the One You Love

Perfection doesn't exist. You have to approach
marriage with a learner's permit to work out your
incompatibilities. It is a continual effort.

—DR. JAMES C. DOBSON

Recently one morning, I read an article in our local newspaper titled "Grow Up! It Might Save Your Marriage" by Steve Cornell, a senior pastor at a nearby Bible church. When I read the title, I laughed, but the reality is that it's true. Someone once said, "Marriage is our last, best chance to grow up." To truly experience the meaningful companionship marriage has to offer, we must think more maturely about it. Part of the problem is that the cultural message has us conditioned to believe that it's our mate's duty to keep us happy. In *How Taking Responsibility Can Make You a Happy Adult*, psychiatrist and family therapist Frank Pittman says, "Marriage is not supposed to make you happy. It is supposed to make you married!" We put unrealistic expectations and pressures on our marriages. Pittman continued, "Marriage is not about being in love. It is about agreement to love one another. Love is an active, transitive verb. It is something married grownups do no matter how they feel."

Philippians 2:3–4 cautions us to do nothing out of selfish ambition or vain conceit, but in humility consider others better than ourselves. Each of us should look not only to our own interests but also to the interests of others—especially our mates Cornell writes, "Marriage offers many opportunities to forsake self-centered and childish ways of living. When couples understand that marriage is not about being in love but about the agreement to love one another, they discover a deeper and richer meaning in marriage."

Agreeing to love also means that we will accept the differences between us. Genesis tells us that the Creator made *two* sexes. It is very important to understand that men and women are unique by design. God designed each gender for a specific purpose. Focus on the Family founder Dr. James Dobson says in *Love for a Lifetime*, "I say to you as husbands and wives, celebrate your uniqueness and learn to compromise when male and female individuality collides." *Compromise*. That's often easier said than done.

PRAYER KEEPS OUR VISION CLEAR

Reading Stormie Omartian's book *The Power of a Praying Wife,* I found it was one of the most powerful books I have ever read. It changed my attitude and my perspective about marriage. It has made compromising a little bit easier because it taught me that only God can change people. It also taught me to grow up and accept responsibility for who I am, and how I have affected our marriage. Caring for my husband took on a completely different perspective when I finally accepted him as he is. If God wants him to be different, then God will have to make the changes. In the meantime, I have learned to pray for him and forgive him. That has made caring for him so much easier. Why? Because my attitude is different.

Omartian says, "Something amazing happens to our hearts when we pray for another person. The hardness melts. We become able to get beyond the hurts, and forgive." Ultimately, forgiveness and prayer is the best way to care for your spouse. Guideposts writer Carol Knapp offered this about her elderly aunt and uncle and how they learned that forgiveness is the secret to a long marriage:

I hadn't seen my uncle and aunt in a dozen years or more, so I was excited to attend a family reunion in California in honor of my Uncle Lokki's eightieth birthday. One evening we were invited to dinner in a neighboring community and stopped along the way for ice cream my aunt had promised to provide. Since my uncle was not entirely certain of the "back door" route to the house from the store, he just started zigzagging every which way, heading toward the general vicinity of a water-tower landmark.

Meanwhile, my eighty-one-year-old Aunt Pat, who had reached our hostess on the cellular phone, found it impossible to direct her determined husband, who was switching streets fast enough to make our heads spin. My mother and I, grinning helplessly in the backseat, further aggravated matters. My aunt got so frustrated that she jabbed Uncle Lokki in the shoulder and sputtered, "I'm not speaking to you the rest of the night!"

We finally arrived at the house, called a truce during the meal and eventually headed home. The sunroof was open to the starry night sky, letting in the mellow summer evening. From out of the stillness my uncle's contrite voice asked, "Have you forgiven me for the way I acted today?"

My aunt responded, "You haven't asked me to."

He paused, took the plunge and respectfully said, "Honey, will you forgive me?" She reached over and squeezed his hand, and it was done.

After fifty-five years of marriage, a loving relationship still comes down to forgiving and being forgiven.

SIMPLICITY MADE SIMPLE

Invite Jesus into your relationship with your spouse. Exercise prayer and invite Jesus to shine His light on your marriage. When decisions need to be made, **SUBMIT TO EACH OTHER AND TO GOD** and ask Him to bring your hearts into agreement with His will and purpose—always agreeing to love each other despite how you feel.

Always **DO WHAT YOU SAY YOU'RE GOING TO DO**. Nothing is more frustrating than to be let down by the one you love. If you say you will spend Saturday cleaning out the garage—then do it! When one partner doesn't follow through on promises, the other partner is relegated to the role of a parent or a nag. That is neither fair nor healthy for your marriage. When people consistently break promises, eventually no one takes them seriously. Worse yet, no one will trust them. Trustworthiness is also about being honest about how you are feeling or what you need. If you're upset about something, don't expect your spouse to read your mind. Be honest and candid. But be tactful, not blameful.

SHOW APPRECIATION. This is especially important in situations where you see people every day. It's easy to get complacent and forget to show or express words of appreciation in the midst of daily living. That can make your spouse feel as if he is being taken for granted. It may seem silly to thank your husband for cutting the lawn every week—but try it. You'll be amazed at how much it will mean.

LEARN TO COMPROMISE. Prayer is critical in times of disagreement. When all else fails, God is the answer. Ask Him to intervene and soften both of your hearts.

Stay connected. Weave your lives together. Look for activities that you both can enjoy. **FIND WAYS TO SUPPORT EACH OTHER.** Even when your spouse is out of town, keep in touch and find ways to be helpful, whether it's simply forwarding his e-mails or doing the research for an upcoming home project.

Develop true, honest and deep compassion for your partner. Janet Luhrs, author of *Simple Loving*, says, "This real kind of compassion enables you to **STEP OUT OF YOURSELF** as if you were watching a movie, and 'be' inside your partner to really understand what life is like for her or him. We all know how truly wonderful and heavenly it is when someone we care about seems to really understand us—even if they don't agree."

> Father, please forgive me when I do not see my partner as You see him. Help me to love my husband just the way he is. Help me to be a true friend who demonstrates how much You care for him. Help me to remember that loving him is a way of showing my love for You. Amen.

Caring for the Everyday Heroes

Do not say to your neighbor, "Come back later;
I'll give it tomorrow"—when you now have it with you.

—PROVERBS 3:28 (NIV)

W ho are the everyday heroes? They are your friends, neighbors, co-workers, pastors, missionaries, teachers, government workers, military, police and your postal delivery people too. Though we seldom think of them as heroes— they are. Just yesterday the UPS deliveryman struggled without complaint as he delivered an oversized, bulky, heavy container. He does this for me on a regular basis. Many of our pastors are overworked and underpaid, and yet are willing to forgo dinner with family if one of their sheep needs a listening ear. Almost every workplace has an "Office Mom." You know who she is. She's the one who always remembers to get the birthday card and take the time to be sure everyone on the staff signs it.

Basically, the everyday heroes are the people who care for us. Now it's payback time—time to start taking care of them. It doesn't take much effort—you simply have to make a habit of thinking about these wonderful people and then caring for them will come easily. I read an article on ChristianityToday.com that was adapted from Kent Humphrey's book *Show and Then Tell*. In it Humphrey spoke about an experience he had at work that makes clear how we can miss amazing opportunities to care for those around us simply because we are focused on other things that keep us from being flexible. Humphrey was conversing with an employee at the office. This fellow had been trying to tell him about a heartbreak he was experiencing with his teenage son. Humphrey rushed to conclude the conversation because he was hurrying to leave the office. He wanted to get to church to fulfill his commitment to go out for a home visitation. As he drove to church, he felt a rock in the pit of his stomach. His heart convicted him to the point of tears. He knew what God was saying, "Ministering to people isn't about activities; they're your life. Start listening and talking to people every day." In other words, don't go talk to someone you don't know when you haven't even talked to the person at the next desk who's crying for help.

There are other ways we can show those we work with that we care. Penelope Trunk, a New York-based writer who has started Internet divisions at Fortune 500 companies, founded two technology-focused companies and endured an initial public offering (IPO), a buyout and a bankruptcy. Her management tip: bake cookies. That's right, bake them at home and bring them into the office. This advice applies to both men and women and requires no great cooking skills. Simply surprise people with your caring and kindness. Trunk says that with a cookie in hand, co-workers will take bad news from you much more generously. "Cookies are a good way to do the most important part of your management job, which is making people around you feel like you care about them. You cannot be a good manager if you don't care about people, and you cannot fake caring about people, or caring about cookies." Great advice!

PRACTICE BEING A HERO FOR OTHERS

Doing business by "the Book" simply means that we make the well-being and continuous growth of our co-workers a very high priority. It also means that we keep confidences. Every workplace has a person who seems to have the low-down on everyone and loves to make it public knowledge. Never, ever reveal anything that you hear from the office gossip trail. Proverbs 11:13 tells us not to be a tale-bearer. This, however, does not give us permission to conceal crimes or serious breaches of ethics. But if a harmful rumor is flying about a co-worker, we should let that rumor stop with us instead of passing it along.

Every person needs to feel that he or she is wanted, included and valued. Whether missionary, pastor, co-worker, neighbor or friend, we all need to know that the people around us love us, respect us, and value our gifts and contributions. We simply need to know that we are appreciated. We need to let those around us know we consider them our "everyday heroes." Perhaps the best way to do that is to begin by reestablishing a place of honor for heroes. Guideposts writer Arthur Gordon shows just how much we trivialize the whole concept of hero:

> My hometown of Savannah, Georgia, is full of monuments to old dead soldiers. The other day, in one of our squares, I noticed a six-year-old standing with his father in front of one of these bronze warriors. "Who's that, Daddy?" the child asked. "Oh, some hero or other," the father replied absently, and the two moved on.
>
> Patriotism. Courage. Sacrifice. Noble virtues, certainly. But I couldn't help wondering if that youngster's concept of a hero

might henceforth be limited to the image of a fighting man dying bravely with sword in one hand and flag in the other.

Then I remembered a letter that came not long ago from a friend in North Carolina, Wayne Cobb. Wayne was talking about heroes in that letter, and this is what he said: "My idea of a hero is someone who is to be cherished not so much for what they have accomplished in their own lives, but for what they have accomplished in mine, for how they have inspired me to grow and to change and to become more of what I was created to be."

That's a much bigger concept, isn't it? Think about it. Who has played such a role in your life? Some wise grandparent? Some quiet schoolteacher? Some understanding neighbor? And think a bit further: Have you played this role yourself? Are you a hero to some other person? Emerson wrote: "Our chief want in life is someone who will make us do what we can." Are you that kind of someone?

If you have had such heroes in your life, why not let them know and thank them? If you doubt that you're a hero to anyone else, why not try harder?

Proverbs 3:28 exhorts us to do acts of kindness, and to be good neighbors by making the emphasis of our lives love and faithfulness. By doing so, we may even become heroes.

SIMPLICITY MADE SIMPLE

CARE FOR THOSE AROUND YOU. There's an old story about a woman who had a chance to be shown hell and heaven. First she was taken to hell, where she saw an enormous banquet room filled with food. As she looked around she saw that all of the people sitting around the banquet table were starving. She noticed that their arms were kept straight by splints that made it impossible for them to feed themselves. "That was truly hell," she thought. Then she was taken to heaven, where she was amazed to find herself in an identical room. There too, the people had splints that prevented them from bending their arms to eat. But the people in heaven were well-nourished and happy. As she examined things more closely, she realized that the difference between heaven and hell is that in heaven they had discovered they could feed each other.

Care for missionaries. The ongoing support of a small church group is critical to the well-being of most missionary families. If you are part of a small group, **CONSIDER ADOPTING A MISSIONARY FAMILY**. Letters, care packages and fund-raisers are great ways to show you care. But be sure to also allow your missionary heroes to be emotionally and spiritually vulnerable so that you may nurture them this way too. Depression and burnout are issues that many missionaries must face, but they don't have to face it alone. When they return home—they may need your care more than they realize. Friends of ours were surprised to find the transition of moving *home* after nine years away even harder than going out to the field. Our small group has been a critical part of their reentry. It has given them familiarity, friendship and love.

CARE FOR THE SINGLE PEOPLE IN YOUR LIFE. Singles need a sense of family. And families need singles. Provide them with a healthy channel for building

CARING CONNECTS
US WITH
GOD'S PLAN

93

relationships so that their intimacy and nurturing needs can be met. Be intentional in including singles in your activities. We have a single (again) gal in our small group. She really appreciates the opportunity to be a part of family activities with all of us.

PRACTICE AFFIRMATION. People need to be appreciated and to be told that their dedication and service are noticed and valued. Make a point to learn the first name of everyone who serves you, such as the coffee server at your favorite coffee shop. Acknowledge the person who delivers your mail with a small token like an apple, an icy drink when it's hot outside or a note of thanks. When people treat you courteously, be sure to thank them.

BE A CARING NEIGHBOR simply by paying attention and making the effort to go the extra mile. If you know some neighbors have been especially busy— surprise them and mow their lawn. If one of your neighbors is ill, offer to sit with her or him so the family can get a needed break. When you've finished snowplowing your own sidewalk—go ahead and do your neighbors' too!

> Lord, I praise You for being able to take little things
> we do and make them big events in other people's lives.
> I also thank You for putting heroes in my life
> who challenge me to live a better life. Loving our neighbors
> is a great idea; thank You for making the rules
> for a good life so simple. Amen.

Caring for All Creation

The Lord God took the man and put him in the
Garden of Eden to work it and take care of it.

—GENESIS 2:15 (NIV)

I moved from the big city of New York to the farming community of Lancaster, Pennsylvania, nearly twenty-five years ago. It was one of the biggest adjustments I have ever had to make. But I have fallen in love with this region of the country and developed an appreciation for the good earth. I love flying home after a business trip to the comforting scene of the patchwork of farms that blanket the surroundings. But the growing population, as in so many other places, threatens our way of life here.

As my small town has become a bedroom community to New York, New Jersey, Philadelphia and Baltimore, urban sprawl and development are seriously affecting the farming community. We are struggling with deciding which priority is more important: farming or the building of houses and the infrastructure necessary to support them. For the farmers the decision can be hard, especially for those who are close to retirement age. Builders are willing to pay millions for a farm. That kind of money will certainly make retirement easier and leave plenty left over for their heirs. I don't know the answer—no one here does. We all care about the farms, but we also are facing the reality of providing for those who live here as well. As we continue to battle this out, it has only made me more aware of our responsibility in caring for God's *creation*.

I choose to use the word *creation* and not *environment* because I think the word *environment* simply doesn't convey the astonishing ability of God and the richness and diversity of the world He created.

Loren Wilkinson is professor of interdisciplinary studies at Regent College. He wrote an article for goodsteward.com titled "Why Christians Should Be Environmentalists." In it he said, "Thinking of the earth as creation helps us, as Christians, to see several truths more clearly. We should rejoice in the fact that so many today are responding to the great, silent 'religious broadcast' of creation. In the Psalmist's words, the message about the glory of God 'goes out into all the earth . . . to the ends of the world.' In their initial, worshipful response to creation, many environmentalists are turning away from the falseness of much in our modern culture. In defending the goodness and integrity of creation they take a step toward the reality of God."

We can pray and have hope that eventually all of us who care about our world will *see God through nature—through creation*—instead of mistaking creation for something so impersonal it loses its sense of glory. Wilkinson said, "We live on a planet whose millions of kinds of living creatures are intricately connected with each other." The whole living earth is God's creation. The problems therein should concern us simply because we are fellow creatures, but particularly because we are persons of faith.

THE EARTH IS A GIFT WORTH PRESERVING

Our task as stewards in Genesis 2:15 was to uphold and preserve God's garden, God's world, and His purposes for creation—all of it—the land, fields, birds, waters, air and space. We were placed here to cultivate and protect it. So, whether you agree with all that the environmentalists say or not, it's still important for you to do your fair share as author Carol Kuykendall did and shares in her story written for *Daily Guideposts*:

> "Anyone have anything else before we close in prayer?" our Bible study leader asked as we sat around a table in the church conference room, sipping coffee from paper cups and finishing our discussion on the first part of Genesis.
>
> Kay timidly raised her hand. "I've been thinking about God's command to 'keep the earth' and wondered if we could bring our own coffee mugs from home instead of using these disposable ones each week. I know it's not *convenient* but it is *obedient*."
>
> We all nodded in agreement, but I felt a twinge of guilt as I fingered my paper cup. Lately I'd read so much about our community's efforts to preserve the environment that I had begun to view the whole ecology movement as a civic responsibility instead of a spiritual duty. When I occasionally got careless about sorting and saving newspapers or tossed an aluminum can into the regular trash, I thought about Uncle Sam, not God. But here in Genesis was the truth: God created the earth and gave it to humankind as a gift, commanding us to take

care of it. God gave me a responsibility and I need to think of everyday ways to respond, like purchasing reusable grocery bags, or picking up a slightly-out-of-the-way neighbor for a night meeting or bringing my own coffee cup. Not always *convenient* but *obedient* . . . to God.

SIMPLICITY MADE SIMPLE

Live reverently and respectfully. Make an honest effort to stop doing damage to creation by overworking and overconsuming. **SEEK THE ABUNDANTLY SIMPLE LIFE.** As individuals we must live with an active awareness of our surroundings and the footprint we will leave on creation. We should also take steps to revitalize the good earth. We should be proactive in our efforts to restore degraded lands and build wildlife habitats amid urban and suburban sprawl.

COMMIT YOURSELF TO A PROJECT. The girls in a local scout troop decided to make a difference by cleaning up and improving a wildlife habitat. They felt they could make a positive impact on an area in need. They focused on two themes: creating homes for animals that live in the park and comprehensive cleanup. The girls built bluebird houses and wood duck, bat and owl boxes at troop meetings. When spring weather arrived, the girls installed the birdhouses and nesting boxes, cleaned up debris in the park, trimmed hedges and cleared trail areas. Taking the project a step further, the girls planted native wildflowers in the park.

Take on a *big* job and **MAKE IT A FAMILY AFFAIR**. Thirty-one boy scouts based in Lancaster, Pennsylvania, spent eleven days at Yellowstone National Park last July where they volunteered to help rid the park of invasive plants threatening native flora. They were joined on the work vacation by nine siblings, twenty-three parents and eleven of the troop's scout leaders, including Scoutmaster Jim Wenger, the seventy-year-old dynamo who has molded boys and shown them a heck of a good time too for almost thirty-eight years. They banished more than one ton of nondesirable plants, estimates Paul Miller, the National Park Service official assigned to work with Troop 99.

Challenge urban sprawl. Why not start a campaign dedicated to slowing development and encouraging **"SMART GROWTH" FOR YOUR COMMUNITY**? Here in Lancaster we are putting forth an effort to change zoning and building requirements to allow more density within our residential communities and add business and retail to the mix as well to encourage people to walk to work and shopping.

BE DILIGENT IN RECYCLING and disposing of your unwanted things. Many churches and civic organizations have "clothes closets" where people may receive needed clothing. Some specialize in children's school clothing. Others provide infant clothing and equipment to young mothers. Thrift shops run by charitable organizations are another option. Household appliances and furniture can be donated to organizations that provide housing for the homeless, group homes for the handicapped and homes for those recently released from prison.

Increase your knowledge and gain a new appreciation for God's creation by **PARTICIPATING IN A LOCAL "ENVIROTHON."** The group here meets once a month beginning in June to plan and organize the event. Study materials, guest speakers and field trips are provided by the steering committee. The program cultivates sensitivity about our limited natural resources and encourages activities and studies that demonstrate concerns for the environment. It also contributes to the protection of the environment and resolution of environmental problems.

> Lord, thank You for this amazing earth and Your perfect design for all creation. Give us wisdom to know how to care for it and the creatures upon it. Convict us of wastefulness and show us new ways to meet the needs of the people, plants and animals that must all share this space. Amen.

PART FOUR

Caring Is an Act of Grace

INEVITABLY, THERE WILL BE A DAY when someone you love will need your help. Perhaps you have already made adjustments in your life in order to facilitate the care of a loved one who is in declining health. This new responsibility can bring with it stress and difficult feelings, both of which are normal reactions. Realizing that occasional dependency is a natural process in the cycle of life may help us prepare for the day when it is our turn to care for someone with special needs. In the next section, I have included many nuggets of wisdom from those who have been effective caregivers. I hope that you will find their insights both helpful and able to lighten your own load when it is your time to care. One of the most important things to remember as a caregiver is to simply do what you must do to remain healthy yourself—this also is a way of loving the one who needs you. Remember, caring is something that God has asked us to do for each other, and He is able to give us the grace we need in order to succeed at what He has called us to do.

Caring for Exceptional People

Therefore, strengthen your feeble arms and weak knees.
"Make level paths for your feet," so that the lame may
not be disabled, but rather healed.

—HEBREWS 12:12–13 (NIV)

A number of years ago as part of my training for designing for those with special needs, I was required to "take on" a different handicap each day. One day Vaseline was smeared on the inside of sunglasses to mimic a visual impairment. I was required to wear them throughout the day. At lunch, I found it nearly impossible to read the menu or the bill. The following day, I was given a wheelchair. I soon discovered that the building where the classes were being held was *not* accessible to those with disabilities. The next day I was given a blindfold and a cane. I was instructed in the use of the long-cane method that many blind persons use to find their way. That was quite a struggle. I needed a lot of help that day. The experience was a good one—it not only gave me "insight" into how to be a better designer for people with special needs, but it also gave me a more compassionate disposition toward them.

When I was growing up, "exceptional" kids were mainstreamed. There were no special classes for them. They were simply part of our class. In fact, each of us learned how to help those students with each of his or her particular needs. One girl was epileptic. We were taught exactly what to do when she had a seizure. Another girl had muscular dystrophy. By the time we reached high school, her condition had deteriorated to the point where she had very little muscle control, which left her without speech, in a wheelchair and downright frustrated. Every quarter a student was assigned to be her "helper." That could be a dangerous job because when this gal was really exasperated, she would manage just enough muscle control to use her arms to fling her textbooks off the tray of her wheelchair and they would fly! But that didn't stop us from caring for her. In fact, I think because we had grown up with her and experienced her decline, we cared more. We had compassion for her and were able to continue to care for her despite her outbursts.

The reality is that none of us is perfect. Some people's disabilities are more obvious than others'. All of us require "extra grace" now and then. In our small group at church, we call that EGR—extra grace required. We all need to recognize that whether the special need is a physical or a learning disability, emotional or behavioral problem, hearing, speech, vision, or language difficulty or trouble in adjusting to life changes, we all have the same basic requirements to live up to each of our potentials and pursue our God-given purpose.

I believe that "exceptional people" have an exceptional purpose. Sometimes, they teach their families to love others better.

There is a large pool of exceptional people whom God has designed for "exceptional" purposes. The church could play an important role in this process. But helping people with special needs fulfill their purpose is often difficult because of our lack of experience. We don't know what to do, so we simply do nothing. That's sad, because with a little education and understanding the church can provide a safe and caring place for all people— especially the exceptional people within our communities. In fact, the church can be a place for those persons to provide a unique perspective of wisdom and spiritual insight for the rest of us. They can be effective team players and capable partners in ministry if given the chance.

Several years ago, there was a young man in our church with a passion for preaching. His speech was difficult to understand and his mental ability limited, but his heart was filled with the love of God. He attended workshops and was encouraged to preach from the pulpit a couple of times a year. Eventually, God provided him with a full-time ministry at a camp for others with special needs.

PROVIDING OPPORTUNITIES

The problem is that too often we simply make people with special needs dependent on us. We limit the amount of work they can do. Caring is a give-and-take relationship. Persons with disabilities want to be included in the caring of the church. They, like you and me, simply want to use their God-given abilities to help others. And what better place for them to do that than in the church?

There are a multitude of ways that people with disabilities can help others: As small group leaders sharing from personal experience about their difficulties and the principles and insights God has taught them; in music and drama to help others express worship; in prayer groups or prayer chains; as class outreach-evangelism leaders; as pastors, ministers of education and music leaders; and as ushers and greeters in worship services. They can also take part in visitation ministry. The list for active participation is nearly endless. But the difference it can make is immeasurable. It is only when we let people who have special needs be a part of things that they will truly feel accepted.

Justin Van Landschoot learned this lesson and wrote about it for Guideposts:

> I have a friend named Jay whom when I first met, I did not know how to treat him. He has been handicapped since birth with mental retardation. He is eleven years old, but acts about three or four even if sometimes he pretends to be older.
>
> Jay's family met our family at St. Johns Collegeville on a sunny afternoon in July. We had planned a picnic and then to go canoeing; we did not know that Jay had never been on a lake or in a boat.
>
> After lunch, my dad and I were going to take Jay in our canoe. However, Jay was frightened that he would fall into the water. I told Jay that I would sing "Row Row Row Your Boat" and hold his hand if he would get into the canoe. Jay did not say anything for several minutes after getting into the canoe; then he began to sing at the top of his lungs "Row Row Row Your Boat." When we got back to shore, Jay told me, "I big person like Justin now."
>
> When I think about how frightened Jay was to get into the canoe, and yet did it because someone took the time to work him through his fear, it makes me believe that when you reach

out to someone and take just a few extra minutes, small miracles can happen.

All of us need a little extra grace now and then. Let's all learn to take better care of each other, including the exceptional people in your life and those that care for them too. Leo Buscaglia, in his book *The Disabled and Their Parents*, says, "When we experience deep pain of an emotional nature, we need to be approached with great sensitivity; we need to be accepted in an upset state; we need to feel we can trust others enough to let down our guard, say what we choose and not be judged or criticized. In fact, the fewer the words, the better; the caring communicates itself without words if it is genuine."

SIMPLICITY MADE SIMPLE

Don't forget that **THOSE WITH SPECIAL NEEDS ARE PEOPLE FIRST**. Buscaglia says, "Remember that persons with disabilities are *persons* first and disabled individuals secondly. These persons have the same right to self-actualization as any others—at their own rate, in their own way, and by means of their own tools. Only *they* can suffer their nonbeing or find *their* selves. They have the same needs that you have, to love and be loved, to learn, to share, to grow and to experience, in the same world you live in. They have no separate world. There is only *one* world."

Remember that people with disabilities, no matter how disabled, have **A LIMITLESS POTENTIAL FOR BECOMING**—not what we desire them to become but rather what God wants them to be. Allow them to find their own manner of doing things. There are many ways to tie a shoe. They must find the best way for them.

TEACH CHILDREN TO HAVE A GREATER UNDERSTANDING of all people. Help them to look beyond exterior appearances to the valuable person inside. When you have the opportunity to interact with exceptional people, use it to help your child to have a more compassionate attitude toward those who happen to look or be different. Point out the similarities instead of the differences. After all, there are so many ways in which we are similar.

GET INVOLVED. Part of caring is a willingness to simply be involved in the lives of other people. Families of persons with disabilities have needs that you can help meet. Use a sensitive approach that recognizes the harsh realities of their lives. Disabilities are long term. They require a long-term commitment. Families of the disabled often feel isolated and limited in finding friends. They lack support and understanding. They experience physical exhaustion, marital problems, financial burdens, grief, anger and resentment. Invite the entire family to your church where they can express their spiritual questions, hurts and frustrations. Church members can also act as extended family in practical ways by offering counseling, financial support and genuine friendship. Offer to take them shopping, invite them to your home or to recreation activities. Learn all you can to truly help with their needs.

BREAK DOWN THE BARRIERS—one by one. Friendship Community here in Lancaster is a nonprofit Christian ministry serving people with developmental disabilities. Through its group homes and community outreach programs, the ministry is improving the social skills of those with disabilities and increasing the understanding of the general public. "Breaking Barriers" is their theme. Those barriers can be attitudes, fears or anything else that keeps people from affirming the worth of those with disabilities and including them as a natural part of our lives. Sheila Myers, director of care support, said, "I think if we take the time, we can learn as much from the people who live in the homes as we think they can learn from us. I've learned more over the years in patience, and in looking at life in a different way."

Lord, I am grateful for the times that You sent help to me when extra grace was required to get me through. I pray for people and families of those with special needs. Help me to be sensitive to ways that I can care for them, and open opportunities for me to also learn from them. Amen.

Caring for Those with Long-term Illness

Is any one of you sick? He should call the elders
of the church to pray over him and anoint him
with oil in the name of the Lord.

—JAMES 5:14 (NIV)

When we are facing difficult trials we need to know how great God is. This is especially important when someone is facing a terminal illness because it can bring peace and the assurance that God is ultimately in charge and will care for us. Assurance that God cares may not provide all the answers to our questions about why things are happening, but it does help us deal with the fear and pain.

The book of James gives detailed instructions concerning prayer for someone who is ill. The sick person should call for the elders of the church who are instructed to pray over him and anoint him with oil. Prayer is the more significant ministry of these two acts performed by the elders; the next verse says, "And the prayer offered in faith will make the sick person well" (James 5:15, NIV).

We can assume that as caretakers we should also be praying. Prayer is a significant application of ministry because it invites God's presence into the situation and reminds us of His greatness.

When I was facing cancer, prayer became my sustaining lifeline. It was then that I learned the true meaning of "praying unceasingly." No matter what else I was doing, my heart was in prayer. My particular cancer—cervical and uterine—did not bring me pain or symptoms that I could see. I had to go completely on faith, trusting God for the outcome. My job was to be obedient in faith and trust Him for His purpose in my life while doing all I could to help myself. That sounds simple, but it was a true and difficult test of faith. Without the loving and constant prayers of those around me, I do not think it would have been possible. When I was too scared or too weak to have faith for myself, their prayers of faith upheld me. They also ministered with wisdom concerning physical and emotional medicines for healing.

The ministry of caring for those with life-threatening and long-term illness is not for the faint of heart. It's a lot of work, a lot of stress and it can leave you depleted and in need of healing yourself. It's complicated because each of us responds to the stress differently. The combination of stress-related responses can make some days an emotional roller coaster. Caregivers can find themselves feeling guilty when they get angry at their patient. If you are in this situation, don't be hard on yourself.

FIND A LISTENING EAR

Long-term illness can bring out intense anger. Out of frustration and fear, the patients will sometimes direct their anger at family members and caretakers.

It's not that they are ungrateful. They are simply in a situation that is bigger than they are at the moment. None of us can predict how we might respond under similar situations. What makes the situation even harder is that what works for one person does not necessarily work for another.

I needed to talk about my illness. It helped me cope. Yet, many of those around me found themselves too frightened by it to engage in a dialog. Instead, they spoke about anything and everything else they could think of. I remember one day, when I burst out with, "I don't really care about the weather!" I wanted to talk about my cancer. That pretty much scared most of them away—which was not my intention—but I was afraid and angry, and needed someone to reassure me that it was okay. That's when I realized that I needed someone to talk to that was not so emotionally involved in the situation. I needed someone who had been there before and could help me find my way through the maze of information—and listen to me without getting upset.

When I found that kind of support, it made the job easier for those caring for me too. Once I was able to safely vent my emotions with outside mentors, it made it easier for me to be less threatening to those who loved me. Each patient and each illness has its own set of needs. We have to realize that it is truly a partnership between the caregiver and the one receiving care. That means the relationship must be healthy for both. And finding the right formula takes time. Evaluating the care needs should be a joint effort and that includes the caregiver being privy to information from the medical staff. It's important to ask your medical team to assess what treatments, adaptations and other changes are necessary.

Even if you are not the primary caregiver but have a friend who is dealing with a long-term illness—there is still much that you can do to be supportive. Guideposts writer Sue Monk Kidd wrote about learning to care for a friend who was dealing with breast cancer:

> Last summer while I was taking drawing lessons, my friend Betty learned she had cancer. The day before she went to the hospital for surgery, her spirit seemed nearly depleted. "What am I going to do?" she said, thinking about the demanding weeks ahead of her. "How will I find strength?"
>
> That evening I found myself doodling on my drawing board thinking of Betty. Soon I was sketching a loaf of bread. A simple, homemade loaf. Then I put it aside and went to bed. But during the night I had the most curious dream. Betty was sitting at a table before a loaf of bread, eating a single piece.
>
> The next morning when I came upon my drawing, an idea began to stir in my thoughts. I reached for my Bible and found the verse, "Behold, I will rain bread from heaven for you" (Exodus 16:4), remembering how day by day God sent nourishment from heaven while His people wandered in the wilderness. There was always just enough for each day. They simply had to trust Him for tomorrow's.
>
> I penciled the verse beneath the sketch of bread and carried it to Betty's hospital room. It was to remind us both . . . when we walk in difficult places, God sends the strength and nourishment to face what comes our way, not all at once, but *day by day*.

Whether you are the caregiver or the care receiver, God is faithful.

ALLOW TIME FOR ADJUSTMENT. Sometimes individuals refuse to believe that something is true. Hope can help. Hope involves accepting reality with an optimistic outlook and taking reasonable steps to make the best of an unfortunate situation. It is important to allow time for them to make the difficult transition from denial to hope.

Face your anger. **IT IS NATURAL TO FEEL ANGRY** about the changes and demands an illness places on a family. It sometimes means a drop in income, new responsibilities and changes in traditional roles. These are practical and emotional burdens that everyone has a right to be angry about. Self-centeredness is also a commonality. I remember feeling betrayed by my body. Feelings and body functions can become the objects of emotional investment. Those being cared for may become angry and critical of those caring for them. They may believe that their situation would improve with a different doctor, a better therapist or a more supportive family. Angry criticism or lack of interest in others easily provokes hurt or anger among family members. We must remember that everyone concerned is adjusting to a new and difficult situation. Most of these feelings will pass with growing adjustment to the disease.

Recognize that helplessness is painful. It makes people feel like a child—weak, frightened and angry. **REALIZE THAT THERE ARE LIMITS TO HOW MUCH ANYONE CAN DO** to help. Some try to help too much, exacerbating the feeling of helplessness. While others simply try to help in the wrong way or at the wrong time. In time, each of you will determine what is best.

Encourage socialization with friends. Some people dealing with long-term illness think that their friends won't understand or won't want to be burdened by their problems. Others worry that friends won't enjoy their company because they are so depressed or preoccupied. But avoiding friends or rejecting their offers to help may actually push them away. **FRIENDSHIP IS AN IMPORTANT SOURCE OF EMOTIONAL WELL-BEING.** Being around others can help restore a feeling of normalcy in an otherwise chaotic time of life.

Go dancing! My friend Adele is a dancer who is recovering from breast cancer. She has started a support group called "Motional Resources." She says that the feedback process between movement and feelings is an innate part of life. Just try vigorously throwing your arms overhead and saying, "I'm so sad." Then fold your arms across your chest and double over, exclaiming, "I'm so happy." Both will feel not only unnatural but also ridiculous. Throwing your arms overhead is exhilarating, and it can accompany a celebratory feeling of accomplishment. Once we understand that movement and experience are inextricably intertwined, **MOVEMENT BECOMES ESSENTIAL TO RELEASING FEELINGS** that are elemental to the healing process. Research is finding that molecular and even genetic changes take place according to how we respond to our experiences. We all move, respond, feel and create. This is the basic belief in this approach to expressive movement; it is inclusive. Everyone can do it. As we incorporate movement and go deeper into our feelings, we can find release.

ALWAYS ASK, "HOW CAN I BE WITH YOU THROUGH THIS?" and then simply listen. Finding out that a friend or relative has a serious illness can leave most of us not knowing what to say or do. Acknowledge how awful the situation is, but be sure to convey a sense of hope too. Don't become a cheerleader expecting the person to act "happy," but do urge that he stay optimistic. Being optimistic is not the same thing as happy. No one dealing with serious illness can be expected to be happy about it. But one can learn to have a positive attitude as much as possible. A positive attitude means hoping to land on the good side of a bad situation. Don't forget to ask what it's like for them. Allow yourself to express your sadness or even cry, but you don't want your friend to feel as if *he* has to comfort *you*.

PRAY. AND THEN PRAY SOME MORE with and for those you are caring for.

Lord, when confronted with illness, I will put my faith in You, my Healer. I will trust You for courage and wisdom to know how to help those who need faith, and I will give thanks for daily bread from heaven to strengthen us. Amen.

Caring for Your Parents

"Honor your father and your mother. . . ."

—EXODUS 20:12 (NIV)

Families have been caring for their elderly parents throughout the ages. What's new is the soaring numbers of elderly people who need care. The fastest-growing segment of the United States population are those over eighty-five. Currently, an estimated seven million Americans are caring for an elderly parent in their homes. And that does not account for the other seven million who are caring for an elderly parent living more than an hour's travel time away. Sadly, most of us are ill prepared to take on this potentially overwhelming task. To make matters worse, our parents aren't ready for it either. And we are all probably dreading it.

Hugh Delehanty and Elinor Ginzler, authors of the book *Caring for Your Parents—The Complete AARP Guide*, say that part of the problem is in how we approach the whole idea of caretaking. "The big mistake that a lot of people make is they look on caregiving as a fix-it project. Here is this weaker person I'm going to take care of. It's going to be a job, like fixing a car," Delehanty writes.

Instead, it is helpful "to look on it as a natural process that's going on between both of you, not just the other person, and then a connection develops. Otherwise, a wall goes up." When viewed in this way, the inevitable role reversal can be rewarding by breaking down generational walls. "I always knew the love was there," says Delehanty. "But I didn't know how much, or how mutual, until my father got Parkinson's and my brothers and I took on new roles in life. Being responsible caregivers changed us all. Toward the end, I realized that I had my father's complete trust. That was a big deal to me."

No matter how we try to prepare, it's always a shock to discover that our parents are no longer able to take care of their own needs. Barbara Deane, author of *Caring for Your Aging Parents* and cofounder of Christian Caregivers, says, "Accompanying the shock of unfamiliar responsibilities is the emotional shock. Watching your loved ones decline in health and strength is painful. Caregiving is painful. Nobody ever tells you that. The hardest pain can be the realization that you may not be able to comfort an aging parent's anxieties and fears. That kind of ache can last forever."[5]

For all that, we can still be encouraged that caregiving is an opportunity for us to grow spiritually. This won't necessarily make it effortless—but then again, those things that mature us rarely are easy. One of the most difficult aspects of caring for our aging parents is deciding when and what to do. It's easy to simply excuse memory lapses, a less than spotless home and other early warning signs, but eventually we will need to assess our parents' capabilities. As we age, we all need a little help. I can no longer expect my seventy-three-year-old mother to get up on a ladder and clean ceilings and light fixtures. At some point, we have to accept the reality that we may be too close to the situation to see it clearly. Barbara Deane suggests praying,

"Lord, help me to see my mother as You see her." How does God see her mother? Objectively, as she really is now. "Learning to accept our parents as God accepts us has a tremendously healing effect on our relationship with them. As you accept your parent, you become better able to accept her feelings."

Relinquishing personal autonomy is seldom done willingly. Determining the proper time and deciding how much independence your parent can safely handle is complex. Unfortunately, despite your best efforts to be kind and sensitive, it is not uncommon for this emotionally charged issue to lead to painfully hurt feelings and misperceptions. Part of the problem is one's perception of the situation, complicated by individual personalities. Logically, it may appear to you that it is time for you to step in and help, but your parent may see your intervention as betrayal, greed or even conspiracy. That's why it is critically important that, unless your parents are mentally incompetent, they should be fully in on all the discussions, and the final choices should be theirs.

ENGAGE HELP WHEN NEEDED

Establishing needs is important in making decisions for care. Are your parents' current living conditions safe and convenient? Will they need seasonal help for such things as shoveling snow or mowing the lawn? These are relatively easy issues to solve. But the more complex aspect has to do with the level of care each will require personally.

Disability experts categorize needs as a way of simplifying this process. They have grouped day-to-day activities into two sets of categories: activities of daily living and incidental activities. The daily living activities are such things as: bathing, dressing, using the toilet, walking safely, eating and maintaining continence. If a parent cannot perform these activities, she cannot live independently. Incidental activities include using the telephone, getting to places beyond walking distance from home, managing money, doing housework and taking medications correctly. These kinds of activities can usually be provided by in-home helpers.

Another obvious thing to consider is the stability of a parent's general health. Age-related health conditions such as diabetes, poor balance, arthritis, etc., may require daily or even twenty-four-hour care. This is where your parent's temperament needs to be honestly assessed. Some people are comfortable depending on others; some are not! If your parent values independence over security, you may have a fight on your hands. Joseph Ilardo and Carole R. Rothman, authors of *I'll Take Care of You,* say, "Self-determination (the right to make all choices about how one lives) must be honored whenever possible. Your care recipient may not want to relocate, or to accept the help you offer."

If it becomes obvious that your parents need help but continue to resist, be strong and enlist the help of others. Approach all the family members to figure out who should be involved in the decision-making process. Organize a family meeting at your parents' home. Delehanty says that at the actual meeting, "The basic key thing is that what you're doing with this conversation is raising issues, not necessarily solving problems. Get the parents to say what's on their minds. Find out if they've thought about how they would like to be cared for, and what their wishes are."

Remember, this is just the beginning of what should be an ongoing conversation with your family. The important thing is to start facing the situation honestly. Too often, denial by parents and children alike can make a bad situation much worse. Facing our fears is half the battle. The solutions will come but only after we know exactly what we are facing.

SIMPLICITY MADE SIMPLE

Don't argue with feelings. Barbara Deane says, "The natural reaction of caregivers is to try to talk a parent out of her feelings. But **ARGUING WITH FEELINGS NEVER WORKS**. Your parent's feelings are seldom under her rational control. She's no more responsible for having them than for developing cataracts, and they won't go away just because you tell them to. However, they may go away if you support her while she struggles with them."

Let them vent. It isn't pleasant, but it is healthy and necessary for your parents to vent their negative emotions. Realize and accept the fact that these **NEGATIVE EMOTIONS ARE NATURAL**. You are not, however, responsible for them. They are not your fault, no matter what your mother or father says. Most experts agree that if your parents are allowed to vent, eventually these negative feelings will fade away.

Act like God. What I mean is that most of us "react" to situations—but God simply acts. He acts according to His nature regardless of how or what we do. He simply loves us no matter how we may react to His love. We cannot ever be perfect imitators of Christ, but we can relate with greater love by **LEARNING TO *ACT* MORE AND *REACT* LESS**. Focus on opportunities for creating a better relationship with your parent rather than dwelling on the problems.

VALUE YOUR PARENT. Avoid speaking to her as if she were a child. Don't scold, blame or correct. Encourage your parents to continue doing what they can and appreciate what they do. My grandmother continued to crochet little things for us. For her birthday, I bought her a box full of skeins of yarn. She laughed, saying she couldn't possibly use it all before she died. But she loved it. And all of her grandchildren were grateful for her lovingly handmade gifts.

DETERMINE WHAT IS REALISTIC when caring for a parent long distance. All the normal issues and stresses surrounding the care of a parent are magnified when your parent lives far away. (The average long-distance family caregiver lives 450 miles away from the person being cared for—roughly the distance from Chicago to Buffalo.) First consider whether or not you can tolerate the physical fatigue that may result from long-distance travel. How will your decision affect your family responsibilities? Realize that no matter how understanding your family is, eventually it will become a burden on everyone. Can you afford the financial cost of being a long-distance caregiver? A Zogby poll reported that an average of 392 dollars a month was spent on travel and out-of-pocket expenses. Respondents also reported missing days on the job, rearranging their work schedules or dropping down to part-time. Can you afford the emotional cost? Some degree of emotional stress, uncertainty and guilt are typical when acting as caregiver to an aging parent—but these feelings are exacerbated when you provide care from afar.

Arrange for two key tasks when caring from far away. **MAKE NONEMERGENCY LONG-DISTANCE CAREGIVING VIABLE** by arranging for someone to oversee day-to-day care. Second, prepare to cope with sudden changes and medical emergencies. Drs. Ilardo and Rothman say, "This requires advanced preparation and planning, including developing a network of emergency contacts and surrogate caregivers." Arrange for an emergency contact near your parent such as a neighbor or friend. Be sure he is willing to check on your parent in case of an emergency, regardless of the time of day or night. Keep this contact information with you at all times.

Arm yourself with information. Assess your strengths and limits and **WORK OUT A PLAN WITH FRIENDS, FAMILY AND OTHERS** who will be your fellow caregivers. Figure out what can be done from a distance such as paying bills or calling insurance agents. Investigate community services that can help fill in the caregiving gaps. AARP recommends contacting the Eldercare Locator at 1-800-677-1116 or www.eldercare.gov. The Family Caregiver Alliance offers these additional tips: Call on a regular basis to show emotional support; identify people living close to your loved one who can help out, such as friends and clergy; think ahead as it is easier to gather information about doctors and finances before something bad happens.

> Lord, I pray for Your blessings on my aging parents. I pray that each moment I have with them will be filled with loving support and expressions of my gratitude for their investment in my life. Guide me in caring for them, show me ways to honor them and let them enjoy all of the days You have appropriated for them. Amen.

Caring for the Dying

And my temptation which was in my flesh
ye despised not, nor rejected; but received me
as an angel of God, *even* as Christ Jesus.

—GALATIANS 4:14 (KJV)

During his visit to the churches of Galatia, Paul was enduring a sickness. Paul commended believers there for not rejecting him even though his condition was revolting. Such caring is what Jesus meant when he called us to serve the homeless, hungry and sick as if they were Jesus Himself (Matthew 35:34–40). Caring for the sick and dying is hard work and it too can be revolting. It can also be scary because it forces us to face our own fears, anxieties and even guilt. Yet, we are commanded to care despite these feelings. "Helping a family member die well, whether that process takes ten years, two weeks or five minutes is the role of a caregiver. It's a process and it's an experience," says Denise Brown, executive director of the Center for Family Caregivers in Park Ridge, Illinois. "It can be one of the most important achievements you'll accomplish in your lifetime."

According to WomenCentral.net, millions of terminally ill patients are being cared for by family members, particularly by wives, daughters and sisters. Seventy-two percent of caregivers are women. Less than twenty percent of patients received additional assistance from paid caregivers. Some of this reflects the impact of efforts to reduce hospitalization and shorten hospital stays. Regardless, families bear a huge responsibility in caring for people who are dying. And many of us are not prepared for such a job. So we must first rely on our faith and accept the responsibility the same way the patients accept their illnesses—slowly by the grace of God.

PREPARE YOURSELF FOR NORMAL REACTIONS

Dr. Robert Buckman, author of *I Don't Know What to Say,* says, "The point is that [for] everyone going through this transition, no matter how old or young, there is a huge task of adjustment, and this is a time when a close friend and relative can be a real help." This is true for the patient and the caregiver. Both will go through a myriad of emotions that will include shock and disbelief, denial, anger, fear, hope, despair and depression. Sometimes it will come in waves. Other times, a single emotion will suddenly appear without warning.

The process is easier to understand if you know what to expect at the three basic stages. A beginning phase is when the person first faces the threat of death; the second is the illness phase when his life patterns become altered by physical decline; and the final phase is when he approaches death. People facing death often go forward and backward in their understanding of what is happening. They may reach a point of acceptance only to revert to denial. Human emotions simply aren't stable—they change as we struggle to comprehend and deal with reality. Some days it's just easier to handle things than others.

For many, the uncertainty of what is happening is one of the hardest aspects to cope with. When my father was diagnosed with bone cancer, he was relieved. He finally could define the seven-year monster that had slowly taken away his health. Now he could prepare for his death. That gave him peace. When he knew he would no longer need to endure hospitals, doctors, nursing homes or therapy, he smiled. That smile of peace lasted to the end. It was a comfort for him. Living with uncertainty was painful, and the years leading up to that eventual peace were difficult.

Almost every patient facing the threat of terminal illness goes through a phase of shock and disbelief. Buckman says the most common symptom of shock is a breakdown in the ability to make decisions. Even relatively simple decisions, like what to order for dinner, become impossible. Simple tasks, like getting dressed or cooking meals, can take forever. Apathy often accompanies this phase. Denial follows. And it can be hard to deal with because it may happen again and again at different stages of the process.

Denial is when the patient simply refuses to take on the illness. She may even believe that the doctors are wrong—that a terrible mistake has been made—suggesting that the test results are not hers. Dr. Buckman points out that denial is a conflict between knowledge and belief. While the patient's mind is telling her that what is happening is real, the emotion of denial is so powerful that she is truly unable to believe the facts. Nonetheless, denial is a normal part of the coping process. You cannot merely tell her to accept reality and move on. That kind of confrontation is of no benefit. She already knows the facts—she just needs time to accept them.

Anger is common with most illnesses, but when facing a terminal illness anger may never go away. For my father, it became a constant companion. That was hard on all of us. Yes, we understood that he had legitimate reasons to be angry—but we wanted him to still be our father occasionally, without the anger. Those kinds of conflicts make it difficult for the patient and the caregiver. Anger can be directed at the entire world, friends, relatives and the caregivers. Anger can even cause patients to blame the doctors for their situations. Their anger may also be directed at God. To blame God for our pain and loss is not unusual. That doesn't mean that we think God is the cause of our suffering, but we simply need to know that He is there with us—to help us combat and deal with this. Feelings of disappointment, rage and guilt are neither rare nor abnormal.

Fear is one of the most natural emotions to feel. Yet many of us think that we shouldn't be afraid of dying. After all, we're, most of us, believers in something larger than ourselves. We are not supposed to be afraid to die. But fear of dying is a combination of not one single fear—but many. When I was dealing with my own cancer, I wasn't ready to die. I turned my anger into feisty determination to live. Ultimately I had to accept the fact that I was not in charge of that decision. I realized then that I was afraid of suffering. I was afraid of not being able to have children. I was afraid of possible physical changes. I was afraid of being a burden. Being afraid of dying is normal. As a caregiver, supporter and friend, you must help the person to talk about what it is that he or she is afraid of. By doing so, you will bring him relief by helping him to process these emotions.

We must all realize that death is never a sign that God has abandoned us. Should we not always be prepared to surrender the gift of this life so that we may claim eternal life through the death and resurrection of Christ? Although caring for dying persons is part of our stewardship, God doesn't ever expect you to do it alone. He is always with us as Carol Kuykendall discovered when a friend was diagnosed with terminal cancer:

> Coming out of church last Sunday, I ran into my friend Harlow whose wife Marj is a hospice patient, dying of cancer. We hugged silently for a moment and then I stood back and asked how he was coping.
>
> "Well," he paused, "I'm trying to be a *practicing* Christian instead of an *observing* Christian these days."
>
> "What's the difference?" I questioned.
>
> "In the midst of a problem, an *observing* Christian merely watches and waits to see what God will do. A *practicing* Christian uses the resources of his faith to find strength and comfort in the middle of pain. Those resources, like prayer and Bible study, are the tools God gives us to make our faith work. Marj and I are using the resource of praying together, which draws us nearer to God and helps us feel His comfort. I still have my weak moments," he admitted, "but when I feel weak, I know it's time to start *practicing* again."
>
> Later, as I walked toward my car, I thought about my own challenges, small in comparison to Harlow's, but still applicable to his solution. Am I an *observing* Christian or a *practicing* Christian? I asked myself. Am I passively waiting for God to do something, or am I actively participating with Him by using the resources of my faith?
>
> What kind of believer are you?

SIMPLICITY MADE SIMPLE

NEVER FORGET THE POWER OF PRAYER. Prayer is the essence of our relationship with God. Even scientists, doctors and nonbelievers can testify to the observable effect it has on patients. Prayer brings relief. God is our Friend, our Guide and our Helper. Simply talking with Him can be very therapeutic for a terminally ill person. God knows us better than anyone else and He is willing to share in our pain and fear and give us hope and peace. Pray for and with those you care for, but encourage them to pray too.

Ask the terminally ill individual how she wants to die. Posing this question is hard, but not only is it necessary, in most cases those we are caring for are simply waiting for us to be ready to ask the question outright. Even if the one you are caring for is cognitively disabled, ask anyway. Denise Brown suggests asking them about their parents' or grandparents' death. Long-term memory is the last to go. Asking about the past often helps to prepare for the future. My dad had very clear ideas about what he wanted. He needed to talk about those plans. But we also needed to be ready to accept them. **TALK TO YOUR MEDICAL TEAM ABOUT WRITING A LIVING WILL.** A friend of mine's mother did this while she was still well enough to make sound decisions. After several surgeries, she finally decided that she didn't want any more. She asked her family not to revive her if something happened to her again. This removed so much guilt from those caring for her.

ENLIST HELP. You don't have to do all the caregiving yourself. There are a multitude of agencies designed to help regardless of your financial resources. Hospice was an enormous help to our family when Dad was dying. Two days a week they sent someone to sit with Dad so Mom could run errands for the afternoon. Those few hours of normalcy made all the difference. The woman who came turned out to be an old acquaintance. She sat with and prayed for Dad each of those afternoons.

CALL YOUR HOUSE OF WORSHIP. They can provide faithful support and companionship in your time of need.

ACKNOWLEDGE YOUR OWN FEELINGS. You too may experience anger and despair as you sympathize with your loved one. You may also experience a range of emotions independent of them. For example, a loved one may have come to terms with his inevitable death—while you still struggle. Sometimes, being a caregiver makes it hard to find time to grieve and work through all the changes a death will bring to your life.

Lord, I want to be a practicing Christian every day.
I don't want to simply observe Your grace, but I want to
let it empower me, to help me through the difficult days
that lie before me as well as the good days that are
in store for me through Your promise. Thank You for
never leaving me or my loved ones, as we look
forward to eternity in Your presence. Amen.

Realizing Life

There is . . . a time to weep and a time to laugh. . . .

—ECCLESIASTES 3:1, 4 (NIV)

Grief. It can be agonizing, overwhelming, debilitating, lonely and faith stretching. Grief has many causes: death of a spouse, loss of a child, divorce, loss of a parent or even losing a job—all can throw you into the painful throes of grief. Everyone handles grief differently. There are those who hold it inside, only expressing it in private, but never showing emotion to the world outside. Others, who grieve openly, release it and let it go. Yet, still others find themselves angry and wanting to blame someone for their despair. There are no rules for grief. Grief is a process that twists and turns around itself. It takes time—sometimes years—for the process to complete. Simply said, it takes time to heal a broken heart.

Beth Witrogen McLeod is a journalist, author, speaker and consultant on aging, caregiving and healing. She says that it is important to understand what grieving entails because misconceptions complicate the healing process. According to the Center for Loss and Life Transition in Fort Collins, Colorado, there are three widespread myths about grief. Myth One: *There is a predictable, orderly plan to mourning.* When people feel they must adopt a rigid timetable for grieving, they don't allow the natural unfolding of a personal experience. We must realize that each of us mourns in a uniquely different way. "There is a huge range of what is 'normal' in the grief process." Myth Two: *It's best to move away from grief rather than toward it.* Mourners must instead give themselves permission to express their anguish. Sadly, society is often impatient with grief and wants survivors to quickly return to normal. The reality is that the process of mourning must be honored—and that means giving it the necessary time to move through all the phases. Most of us need about a year. Some, much longer. Myth Three: *Following the death of your loved one, the goal is to "get over" your loss.* This belief suggests a total return to a previous vision of normality. Grief transforms everyone at some level. To assume that life can or will be exactly as it was is unrealistic and potentially damaging. Total recovery is not possible. But learning to integrate the loss and move forward is surely possible. *Realizing life*—a new life—is the simple message that can help all mourners cope with loss.

McLeod also says that the event of loss is a transition in life with both an ending and a beginning. "Moving on involves coping with the pain and grief, reestablishing priorities, and refocusing on what truly matters." Anyone who hopes to help another through this difficult process must understand that learning to live again is not an easy thing to do. As we learn to share each other's pain, we can focus on the promise of life and together find ways of coping, honoring and living the life God has for us, just as Ellen Secrest wrote for Guideposts:

One evening, my husband Glenn slipped a paperback book onto my lap. It was titled *Kicking Your Stress Habits* by Donald A. Tubesing, PhD. "Why don't you take a look at this?" he suggested. "I just finished it, and I think it could help you feel better too."

These last few months hadn't been easy. We had just moved to a new state and said good-bye to dear family and friends, our daughter Lauren had moved south for a new career and worst of all, Glenn had lost his job in a corporate takeover. We were in crisis, and I hadn't even acknowledged it.

I thumbed through the book and stopped, puzzled, at a chapter on grief. That had nothing to do with how I was feeling. Stress, yes. But *grief*? Not me. I read that "Grief is the process of healing from the pain of loss. If you've ever had to say good-bye then you've experienced grief." Well, I certainly had said a lot of good-byes recently. "If you short-circuit the healing process by refusing to acknowledge your suffering," states Dr. Tubesing, "you will compound your distress." Otherwise, our buried feelings can show up as depression, insomnia, irritability, even sickness.

Now I better understood the enormous stress Glenn and I were under. We talked to each other about our feelings, cried, lent support when either of us had very tough days. Slowly, we were able to come out of our crisis. We thanked God the day Glenn found new work, and looked forward to visits from Lauren and our friends and relatives.

Have stress—and grief—been disrupting your life recently?

Here are some suggestions for handling grief in a healthy way from Dr. Tubesing's book. Maybe they'll help you as much as they helped Glenn and me.

1. *Allow yourself time to grieve.* Expect this to be a painful time; try not to fight it.
2. *Make new goals for yourself.* Give yourself something to look forward to.
3. *See the loss as an opportunity* to strengthen your faith.
4. *Reach out to others* for comfort—a support group might help ease your pain.

SIMPLICITY MADE SIMPLE

START A JOURNAL. Regardless of the cause of your grief, keeping a journal as you move through the process will help. Dawn J. Lipthrott, a licensed counselor and director of The Relationship Learning Center, encourages those in grief to write, and even draw, their feelings and thoughts. She says to write letters to your pain, anger, sadness, depression, God, loneliness, sexuality, to your past relationship, to the future, to your fears and to your strengths. She also says it's okay to write 'poor me' letters and poison pen letters saying all the bad things you wish would happen—for example, when you are deserted by a spouse. Write love letters, pouring out the love you had and shared. But also remember to write a letter describing the gifts and blessings in your life right now.[6]

TALK TO AN EMPTY CHAIR. It may sound silly, but it works. Place a chair in front of you and imagine the person you want to converse with sitting there. It may be your lost loved one, your long gone parent, a childhood friend or even God. Talk to this person, saying everything that you want to say at that time. Yell, blame, whatever—it's a simple-sounding technique that helps us to process our emotions, and to ease our way into the new life in which we have found ourselves.

GET UNSTUCK. Most people going through grief will encounter a period when they feel stuck. Lipthrott suggests taking a walk and simply counting every object your eyes find—trees, bugs, anything you happen upon. Then as you focus your attention again on the objects around you, instead of counting, say something to them. Example: "You are a stupid tree just sitting there doing nothing!" The point of this is not so much that you have any particular insight, but that you begin to move your attention outward to the world around you. Focusing on things outside of yourself helps you step out of being stuck with your troubling internal thoughts.

ALLOW YOURSELF PRIVATE GRIEVING TIME. Create a specific time when you can be alone to look through mementos and let yourself feel what you feel and express it. You may want a friend in the house, but in another room, so that you can feel free to vent what you need to. Your friend should be there simply for support in case you need it.

SEE A COUNSELOR. When I was going through my divorce, I would never have gone to a counselor if a friend, who had also been divorced, hadn't made me go. It was the best thing for me. Without the caring, professional help of my counselor, I may never have fully processed my experience, and been able to move on to a new and healthier life.

ASK FOR HUGS. Those who are grieving need someone to hold them. This is especially true for those who have been widowed or divorced.

Accept the fact that "happily ever after" is only something to be found in fairy tales. Real **HAPPINESS IS A MOMENT-BY-MOMENT CHOICE**. It's a choice that comes from the depth of your soul. Life will always have its ups and downs. How you choose to respond to each of them is your decision.

Father, I realize that grief is a natural process of loss, and the greater the happiness that someone gave me, the greater the sorrow is when I lose him. I am thankful for those who brought happiness to my life, and I still grieve their loss whenever I think of them. But I will trust that You have more happiness in store for me. From this day forth I will celebrate those whom I miss by embracing those You bring into my life. Amen.

Caring for the Caregiver

When you pass through the waters I will be with you,

and through the rivers they shall not overwhelm you;

when you walk through the fire you shall not be burned

or scorched, nor shall the flame kindle upon you.

—ISAIAH 43:2 (AMP)

Barbara Deane, cofounder of Christian Caregivers, calls this verse from Isaiah 43 "the Crucible of Caring." Caregiving can sometimes seem like a long walk through fire. No matter who you are or how you came to be a caregiver, you are no stranger to stress, exhaustion, isolation, depression and anger. Today, this tough job is falling to one in five of us. Every family will face this in some degree with at least one family member. As caregivers wear out and fall victim to the stress, depression, financial burdens, physical strain and loss of friends, they must learn to take care of themselves before things get even worse. Researchers say that stress on the caregiver can breed violence or neglect. More than half of the abuse experienced by people with disabilities comes at the hands of family members and caregivers, particularly those living together.

Sadly, nearly forty percent of caregivers say no one else provides any unpaid help to the person in need. In addition, most caregivers also have someone else in their lives, such as a spouse or child, to help care for too. The most frequent complaints made by caregivers are not having enough time for themselves, and the difficulty of managing emotional and physical stress and balancing work and family responsibilities. Most feel isolated and trapped. And many found themselves in the position of caregiver without any warning or time to prepare, like my friend Thomas. His wife fell victim in January to a massive stroke that has taken all but a shell of her life. Now, in a permanent vegetative state, doctors have little hope for her recovery. In fact, they said that there is a seventy percent chance that she could have another stroke at any time. Thomas has lost eighty-two pounds in four months. His life changed so drastically that he hasn't even had time to figure out how he feels. He said, "After forty years of marriage, I suddenly can no longer come home and tell Chris about my day." Unfortunately, because Thomas is a man, his situation as a caregiver is even more difficult; most of the support groups are designed for women caregivers.

Caring for yourself is of utmost importance to the task of caregiving. If the caregiver is not healthy and happy, the quality of care may suffer. Deane says, "If you're now walking through His fire, it's a refiner's fire meant to purify you (Malachi 3:2). What are the benefits He intends to bring you in the caregiving experience? (1) A closer relationship with Him, achieved through trusting; (2) a more mature faith, purified by testing; (3) the ability to face and deal with your negative emotions, such as anger, resentment, guilt, fear, anxiety, and sadness, etc., instead of running from them; and (4) healing of your past hurts (and even the healing of entire families). Right now, the most important questions in your life are: 'Can I really trust God to do all this? Really trust Him? Trust Him enough to let Him control me during the caregiving experience?'"

We must learn to recognize who we are allowing to be the controlling force in our caregiving situation. As persons of faith, we should only give up this control to God. Yet, when caring for parents it is easy to let them gain control by making you feel guilty if you don't please them. Even society's expectations can control what we do—we don't want to look like bad, unappreciative children—and we take on more than we can handle in caring for a parent. Or it may be our own egos—the need to be needed—that forces us into acting like martyrs, not allowing others to help and not caring for ourselves. There are so many forces that can manipulate us into not letting God be in control.

We need to find God's perspective for our situation. God expects us to help others, but that doesn't mean we must shoulder all their burdens for them. Galatians 6:5 (NIV) says, "For each one should carry his own load." Everybody is given his own life to live and his own burdens and sorrows. They are his alone. Deane says, "You can help your parent with the burdens of his old age, but you can't be old for him." When we lose sight of this we take on inappropriate guilt and that leads to inappropriate behavior. The only way to break the chains of all these outside forces is to simply stop trying to please our care-recipients and please God instead. Deane says, "The key is to look to God for your approval." The approval of other caregivers who understand can also help you to give up the need for your care-recipient's approval as Guideposts writer Sharon Foster found out in her discipleship group:

"It just seems like I'm always doing this. I'm always the one," Max says.

The women—Max, Theresa, Darlene and Ruth—sit in the circle we share every Tuesday morning. It is my discipleship class, a circle where we meet to pray, study and share our lives. The class is made up of all ages and both sexes. This group, however, is all middle-aged women—some more middle-aged than others.

The four women are discussing caretaking—providing comfort for relatives and elderly parents. Most times the women smile but sometimes there are tears, and they feel overwhelmed and alone. Sometimes they are resentful of brothers and sisters, aunts and uncles who seem to be absent and not sharing the responsibility. The resentment doesn't last long, a momentary but necessary venting. Then Max, Theresa, Darlene and Ruth are back to stories of how they have grown and been blessed by their service. And of how they have learned not to judge those who are not caretakers.

"I wouldn't do it any other way," Max and Ruth agree.

"I was there at her side when my mother passed," Theresa says. "It was an honor." The other women nod in agreement.

Darlene, who has quit her job to stay home with her dying mother, thanks the other women for their wisdom and their generosity in sharing their stories. Their words strengthen her, she says. I watch and listen, blessed by their examples.

SIMPLICITY MADE SIMPLE

Don't become embittered. Anger and guilt are normal emotions for care-givers. You are important to your patient but you also have an obligation to yourself. The most responsible and loving thing to do is to **STAY MENTALLY AND PHYSICALLY STRONG**. That sometimes requires accepting your limitations and finding professional help for those you are caring for. Alzheimer's is a particular situation that can be very difficult to handle alone at home. My granddad did a great job—most of the time managing my grandmother who suffered with Alzheimer's. But when she became violent, he had to come to terms with placing her in a care unit that was able to keep her safe, despite the fact that he felt guilty because he had promised to always care for her. He finally accepted the fact that caring for her *was* exactly what he was doing when he chose an appropriate facility to manage her care.

Stay healthy. **EAT A BALANCED DIET.** Avoid my friend Thomas' crash diet. No one can live on tea and toast alone. Do your best to include the basic food groups in your daily diet. Consider calling Meals on Wheels. It's a great option for getting a home-cooked meal without all the work.

Take time to look after yourself. **TRY TO GET TIME FOR YOURSELF** to do things that you find relaxing and enjoyable. Organize "respite" care for your patient. Respite care can simply be having a friend or neighbor come over for a half hour so you can take a walk outside. Consider using one of the agencies that provide respite care such as home health agencies, social services, private nursing companies, senior centers, churches or the National Family Caregivers Association. When my dad was ill, hospice provided someone to come twice a week. At one point, Medicare provided two weeks of nursing home care for Dad just because my mother was exhausted and needed time to rest.

Focus on the positive and remember that God has promised to always be with you. Allow Him to work in your life through this experience. **FIND AN ENCOURAGING AND SUPPORTIVE GROUP** to help instill His hope in you. Honest interaction with other caregivers will help you develop wisdom in caring for yourself and your care-recipient. Be open to laughter. A lot of amusing events often take place around a patient. It's okay to laugh.

De-stress. The *Caring for the Caregiver* guide sponsored by Parke-Davis suggests the "Heavenly Stretch." They say this **EXERCISE CAN HELP EASE TENSION** during the day. Simply find a quiet place, stand straight with feet together and eyes forward. Exhale. Then inhale slowly and stretch your arms as high as you can. Lift up your toes and reach skyward as you imagine a thread running up through your spine pulling you up. Reach and reach some more! As you reach, continue to inhale slowly as long as you possibly can. Then exhale slowly, slowly. As you let your arms descend slowly, flex your wrists and push palms downward.

Get support for yourself. Acknowledge that **IT'S OKAY TO SEEK SUPPORT**. You may need help or advice to learn how to do something for your patient. Or you may need support to handle the physical, emotional or psychological drain that can affect you as a result of caregiving. Caregivers report that support groups make a real difference in reminding them they are not alone.

Father, when I am caring for those who need my help,
I will remember that You are pleased with the time I am
contributing to their lives. I will remember that there
is no greater way to serve You than to care for those
who are sick or imprisoned by life's circumstances.
I will also enjoy the moments that are set apart for
caring for myself, knowing that times of inner
strengthening will make me more alert to serving
the one in my care, and thus my caring for You. Amen.

PART FIVE

Caring Opens the Windows of Heaven

FAITH WITHOUT WORKS IS DEAD, which means that if we are not willing to roll up our sleeves and help people, our faith is not fully alive. But prayer should always precede action so that we will have wisdom to know what God wants us to do for people. In this last section, you'll find ways to give spiritual care to our loved ones, but the basic fact remains: Only God is the Ultimate Caregiver of us all. When the Lord's disciples asked Him how they should pray, Jesus taught them the Lord's Prayer. We can pray this same prayer for others by simply saying, "Our Father who art in heaven, hallowed is Your name. May Your kingdom come and Your will be done in the lives of those You have entrusted to my care. Give my loved ones the daily bread of Your Word to guide them. Help them to forgive others as You have forgiven them. Lead them not into temptation, but deliver them from evil. For Yours is the kingdom, and the power, and the glory forever. Amen."

Prayerful Caring

Don't worry about anything; instead,
pray about everything. Tell God what you need,
and thank him for all he has done. If you do this,
you will experience God's peace, which is far more
wonderful than the human mind can understand. . . .

—PHILIPPIANS 4:6–7 (NLT)

Cheri Fuller wrote in her book *When Families Pray* about a young man named Jay with Down's syndrome and how his prayers brought peace to his grandfather who suffers from Alzheimer's disease. His grandfather felt lost, confused and disoriented to the point of tears. In addition to Down syndrome, young Jay had a deteriorating heart condition and a speech disability. But this did not inhibit him from effective praying. As he watched his grandfather begin to cry, he got up from playing, placed one hand on his grandfather's shoulder, and lifted his other hand to heaven. In his own words, unclear perhaps to those around him but perfectly clear to God, Jay asked God to heal his grandfather and ended his prayer with, "Thank You, God. Praise You, Jesus." Moments later, a smile came over his grandfather's face as clarity returned to his mind, giving him the ability to suddenly recognize everyone in the family. That's just one example of the power of prayer.

A study conducted at St. Luke's Hospital in Kansas City, Missouri, concluded that intercessory prayer indeed makes a difference. "Prayer may be an effective adjunct to standard medical care," says cardiac researcher William Harris, who headed the study in 1999. The patients all had serious heart conditions and were randomly assigned to two groups. Half received prayer for four weeks from five volunteers who believed in God and the healing power of prayer. The other half received no prayer. Those praying were only given first names of their patients and never visited the hospital. The patients did not know they were being prayed for. The group receiving prayer fared eleven percent better than the group that didn't.

Dr. Herbert Benson, an associate professor at Harvard Medical School and coauthor of *Timeless Healing: The Power and Biology of Belief*, says, "More and more physicians are coming forward to discuss the power of prayer in physical healing because we've seen the power of belief." Benson's surveys showed that nine out of ten Americans say they pray and ninety-five percent of those who pray believe that some of their prayers have been answered. Lois Matson, a hospital chaplain and vice president for Christian Life Ministries, says, "I have spent many hours in hospital ministry meeting with patients and families at the bedside. When physical healing does not take place, prayer is like a comforting warm blanket to the recipient of the prayer. The families feel that something is being done for their loved one when medicine can do no more."

PRAYER ALWAYS MAKES A DIFFERENCE

Prayer is healing, comforting and has the ability to guide us when we are lost. None of this should surprise us; after all, the Bible is clear about the need for and the power of prayer. Sadly, research indicates that the average Bible-believing Christian spends less than four minutes a day in prayer. The question is why? Why do we find it so difficult to commit to prayer? Dr. Bob Beltz, who wrote *Transforming Your Prayer Life*, believes it's simply a matter of obedience. Philippians 2:12–13 (NIV) says, "Therefore, my dearfriends, as you have always obeyed—not only in my presence, but now much more in my absence—continue to work out your salvation with fear and trembling, for it is God who works in you to will and to act according to his good purpose."

"It is a combination of what God does and what we do. God *is* at work *in* you. He is the great motivator, enabler and empowerer. But what God is working within needs to be worked out by our actions of obedience," says Beltz. Simply put, we need biblical willpower and that involves the exercise of our will to act, combined with dependence upon God's power to enable us.

Beltz continues, "In developing a discipline of prayer, the first step is to come to the Lord as the disciples did and to ask Him to teach us to pray." Christ's example of an effective prayer life is the perfect model for us to follow. He would rise before dawn and go off alone to pray. Other times, He prayed all night. Sometimes, He sent the disciples on to their next destination while He remained behind to pray. When the disciples asked Jesus to teach them to pray like Him, He taught them the Lord's Prayer.

Prayer also requires us to act. James 2:17 says that faith without works is dead. Prayer combined with physical action is the one-two punch that makes our prayer life more powerful by demonstrating our faith to those who see us. Our actions give witness to our faith in prayer. Fred Bauer wrote this for Guideposts about keeping faith and works in balance:

> "The polite part of speaking with God is to be still long enough to listen," wrote Ruth Graham in her perceptive book, *Legacy of a Pack Rat*. And sometimes when she listens: "God says, as it were, 'Why are you praying? Do something!'" She went on to quote C. S. Lewis who in the same vein wrote, "It is so much easier to pray for a boor than go and see him."
>
> The Bible tells us to pray without ceasing (1 Thessalonians 5:17), but it also informs us that faith without works is dead (James 2:17). I suspect James uttered the latter to keep the superpious from using prayer and meditation as a dodge from involvement—visiting the sick, lifting the fallen, clothing the poor, sheltering the homeless, feeding the hungry, nurturing the young, listening to the lonely, assisting the old. . . .
>
> How do we keep those two things—faith and works—in balance? One way is to set aside a regular period during the day for both. Not that they are mutually exclusive. Brother Lawrence (who wrote *Practicing the Presence of God*) encouraged engaging in prayer and work *simultaneously*. While the saintly monk was washing pots and pans, standing at a monastery sink, he prayed, which may be the ideal solution for people who are always on the run.
>
> To my knowledge there is no correlation between our posture and the potency of our prayers. Otherwise, Christ would

have insisted that His disciples get on their knees and close their eyes when praying. If I read my Bible correctly, God's focus is on our heart condition, not our body position.

Matthew 16:19 (MSG) says we will have "complete and free access to God's kingdom, keys to open any and every door: no more barriers between heaven and earth, earth and heaven. A yes on earth is yes in heaven. A no on earth is no in heaven." All we have to do is pray and believe and make prayer a partner in our caring for others.

S I M P L I C I T Y   M A D E   S I M P L E

DON'T EVER GIVE UP. The prophet Habakkuk was like many of us. He was concerned about what he was seeing and wasn't sure how God would respond. "What's God going to say to my questions? I'm braced for the worst. I'll climb to the lookout tower and scan the horizon. I'll wait to see what God says, how he'll answer my complaint" (Habakkuk 2:1, MSG). Ed Gray, author of *Forty Days to a Life of G.O.L.D.*, uses the acronym H.E.A.R.T. (Higher Empowerment Abides Resourcefully Therein). He says we must decrease our thoughts so that we can hear God's answers. "As our thoughts decrease, God tells us what to pray for. What God speaks we should write down in our prayer journals. By writing your prayers down, you can read them while you are in pursuit of God's vision for your life."

PRAY FOR OTHERS. I experienced the prayer of a stranger recently as I was on a book tour to ten cities across the country. I was weary and it must have shown on my face when a perfect stranger asked if she could pray for me. God sent this prayer warrior to encourage and lift me up. In the midst of a busy airport, this stranger was a blessing that brought peace and strength as I continued on my journey. Later that evening, the cabdriver who was taking me to my hotel realized I am a Christian and asked if I would bless him with a prayer. I did not hesitate, but I was surprised that he would ask. I prayed for many blessings on his head knowing that God was clearly watching and caring for all of us from above.

PRAY FOR DIRECTION. Gray says, "God almost always gives you directives on how to bring about what you are praying for. As God speaks ideas to you, remember to write them down in your prayer journal and diligently implement those ideas.

When Jesus said in Luke 11:9 that if you knock, the door will be opened to you, He did not mean that your goals would be attained with one simple action. The word *knock* in its Hebrew root is *daphaq* and means 'to press severely.' The fact is, to make something happen, you have to press severely." Knowing this should encourage us when the going gets tough. One of the reasons Christ came to earth was to show us how to **OVERCOME OBSTACLES BY RISING ABOVE THEM**—pressing on severely.

MEDITATE AND LISTEN. In *How to Listen to God*, Charles Stanley says, "When we meditate upon the Lord, we see things from a different perspective. The things that worry us lose their grip. The things that weaken us, God turns into strength. Our inward look at problems or situations is replaced by a heavenly view, because we learn that we are seated in the heavenly places in Christ Jesus."

Lord, forgive me for not asking for Your help in all things as Your Word teaches what we should do. Help me learn to pray without ceasing, keeping my expectancy on You all day long so that I will be quick to hear Your voice when You want to guide me in the way I should go. I want to practice Your presence, and be ready to pray for others who need Your power in their lives. Amen.

Caring and the Great Commission

"Therefore go and make disciples of all nations,
baptizing them in the name of the Father and of the Son
and of the Holy Spirit, and teaching them to obey
everything I have commanded you. And surely I am
with you always, to the very end of the age."

—MATTHEW 28:19–20 (NIV)

Discipleship and mentoring are not an option, but a command. Being a disciple must encompass more than just trusting Christ for salvation. Our acceptance of Christ as Savior is only the beginning. We are called to make disciples—not only to lead others to Christ but to equip them as well so they too can go out to reach and teach others.

The key to accomplishing true discipleship is humble obedience. Richard J. Krejcir of Into Thy Word ministries put it this way, "Humbleness is characterized by the willingness to grow in Christ, and receive learning and experience growth.

Peter tells us we ought to be humble toward one another so that we can know the grace of God and not be in opposition to God. Then secondly, he says, we had better be humble, not only toward one another, but toward God. This is so straightforward. This is so essential to be a blessed church, to be a growing church, not in numbers, but in discipleship."

Yet, many of us hesitate to evangelize others. In fact, we may even have trouble using the word "evangelize" because it sounds like something only pastors and preachers should be doing. Part of the problem is that a lot of us don't even know how to explain our own faith clearly enough for others to understand. We are afraid that people will ask questions that we cannot answer. Part of this fear may come from a lack of training, but part of it can also be a result of "misplaced faith."

SIMPLY TELL OTHERS WHAT YOU HAVE SEEN GOD DO

Our faith to witness cannot be in our ability to persuade but rather in the power of God, His Word and His work. We must remember, as Bill Bright, founder of Campus Crusade for Christ and author of *Witnessing without Fear: How to Share Your Faith with Confidence*, says that "successful witnessing is simply taking the initiative to share Christ in the power of the Holy Spirit and leaving the results to God."

When we accept the fact that God is the initiator as well as the means to salvation in a person's heart, we can relax and follow His command, knowing that He will prepare the hearts of those we speak with. Only He can draw them close and give them the desire for more spiritual knowledge. Our goal is simply to share our testimony of how faith in Christ has changed our lives and to give them a better understanding of the Gospel along with a positive impression of who Christians really are. After all, it may be the only opportunity they ever have for hearing about the "incredulous joy of salvation," as Elizabeth Sherrill called it, in her story about teaching teens in Africa:

"Mrs. Shallow"—it was as close as the sixteen-year-old African boy could come to Sherrill—"will you tell us again about winter?"

Fifty pairs of eager eyes focused on mine. We'd finished the geography lesson and now it was Conversation Time in this earth-floored school in Uganda where John and I and our three children were spending a year of missionary outreach.

Five mornings a week I taught in this wall-less structure where a tin roof on poles kept the equatorial rain from our heads, if not the mud from our feet. During the geography lesson weeks before, the subject of seasons had come up. "During winter where I live," I said, "water turns to ice." I pointed to Lake Victoria shimmering beyond the banana trees. "Lake water becomes so solid you can stand on it."

From then on there was no other subject for Conversation Time. Over and over the young people asked to hear how rain would come down white and slow, how water became hard. Now, looking over the rows of expectant faces, I realized that the topic, for them, had the appeal of a fairy tale. How could I get across the reality of "cold" here on the equator?

Of course! The house we were renting had a refrigerator with an ice-cube unit. . . . Next day I wrapped the ice tray in newspaper and hurried it to school. Handing around the cubes, I saw in the students' faces first shock, then wonder, then the incredulous joy of sheer discovery.

I made a discovery for myself that day. This is *why* we share our personal experiences of God. By passing on what we know to be true, we allow others to touch a portion of that great Reality they never may have encountered before.

If your faith is solid enough to stand on—share it. You never know who may need the miracle of solid water (faith) today!

SIMPLICITY MADE SIMPLE

PRAY FOR OPPORTUNITIES TO SHARE. And pray for specific people, asking God to give them a hunger for spiritual knowledge. When an opportunity presents itself, acknowledge your complete dependence on God and praise Him for what He is about to do. Then proceed with joy, knowing that He is in control of the situation.

USE AN EVANGELISTIC TOOL. Conversation may work well in one-on-one situations, but you may find using a visual aid or pamphlet useful in helping people understand and remember what you are saying. Dr. Bright has a pamphlet entitled *Would You Like to Know God Personally?* (available through New Life Publications, 1988) that is very effective. It has helped many people understand how to simply receive Christ.

Salvation is a heart and head agreement. "Receiving Christ is like a marriage ceremony. Agreeing intellectually that someone is a good mate, or admitting deep emotional feelings, does not make you married. It is not until you say 'I do' as an *act of the will* that you are truly married." So don't be afraid of questions. Unless someone can intellectually, as well as spiritually, accept salvation, it will not happen. **GIVE HONEST ANSWERS TO HONEST QUESTIONS.** To do that you must be willing to do the work or research necessary to give another person the answers he needs so that his faith can be released to surrender to Jesus. A friend of mine asked me some very tough questions when we first went to war with Iraq. I spent a lot of time in my Bible looking for answers. After several hours and much research, I was able to answer at least some of her questions. Despite my inadequacy, she found my faith and my knowledge of it enough to satisfy her. She has not yet accepted Christ, but at least she is asking questions. And that is a good place to begin. And I appreciated her giving me yet another opportunity to share my faith with her. I pray we will continue to dialog.

Be assured the Holy Spirit is present and working. It is not your job to save people—only to **INTRODUCE THEM TO THE TRUTH.** The Holy Spirit will do the rest. A music leader I know, Matt Goss, wrote the following song. I have found it to be a powerful prayer for helping me to be courageous in speaking the truth to those whom God puts in my path. Perhaps you, too, will be encouraged by it.

"Overflow"
by Matt Goss

Verse:
Open my eyes so I can see Your glory.
Open my ears, to hear Your voice more clearly.
Open my heart, Lord, and let it beat with Yours.

Bridge:

Fill me up so I can be poured out.

Fill me up so I can be poured out.

Fill me up until I overflow with You.

Chorus:

Overflow in me, Jesus.

Overflow in me.

Pour Your Spirit out, Jesus.

Overflow in me.[7]

Father, I pray that You will give me opportunities
to tell people what I have seen You do in my life.
I realize that conviction is up to You, but I also
understand that people can't believe if they haven't
even heard about You. Anoint me to share good news
of all the prayers You have answered for me
with people whom You bring across my path. Amen.

Caring Ministries

Carry each other's burdens,

and in this way you will fulfill the law of Christ.

—GALATIANS 6:2 (NIV)

I love this verse because it is the perfect example of practical spirituality. Paul tells us that we are to bear one another's burdens. We are to share the load whenever temptations oppress us or life depresses us. Paul deliberately returns to the thought of love being the fulfillment of the "law of Christ," for loving one another is the new commandment that Christ gave to us (John 13:34). Paul encourages us to take on each other's burdens in mutual sympathy as an act of love.

One of the most effective ways of practicing this kind of caring is through the Stephen Ministries. Stephen Ministries was started in 1975 by Dr. Kenneth Haugk in St. Louis, Missouri. The name *Stephen* comes from St. Stephen, who was the first layperson commissioned by the apostles to provide caring ministry to those in need, as recorded in Acts 6.

The early church leaders took seriously the combination of spiritual and material concerns in carrying out their God-given ministry. They stressed prayer and the proclamation of the Word, but never to the exclusion of helping the poor and needy. The early believers saw church ministry as including various aspects that would encompass all ministry as critically important to the work of the church. Luke's narrative suggests that to be fully biblical is to be constantly adapting traditional methods to create ministries designed to meet any situation, both for the welfare of the whole church and for the outreach of the gospel.

I think Haugk's own words in his book *Don't Sing Songs to a Heavy Heart* express the meaning of Galatians 6:2 most beautifully: "The fragile vulnerability of those who are suffering is what made me so determined to research these concepts of caring and relating. The subject matter, but more importantly, the people who are suffering deserve it. There's more than enough pain in the world to go around. I wanted to alleviate some of that pain by heading off the hurtful and promoting the helpful."

The signature verse for Haugk's book is Proverbs 25:20 (NIV): "Like one who takes away a garment on a cold day, or like vinegar poured on soda, is one who sings songs to a heavy heart." This proverb describes an all-too-human problem each of us faces from time to time. When a friend, neighbor, co-worker, relative or someone else we know is experiencing suffering, we want to help; but our well-intended words or actions often end up adding to the person's burdens instead of easing his or her pain.

Stephen Ministries is in the business of equipping people to do a better job of caring for each other. Congregations and lay caregivers provide one-on-one Christian care to the bereaved, hospitalized, terminally ill, separated, divorced, unemployed, relocated and others facing a crisis or life challenge.

They have been so successful that there are now over 450,000 trained Stephen ministers across the country. More than a million people have received care from a Stephen minister in a formal one-to-one Stephen Ministries caring relationship and millions more have received care from Stephen ministers in informal ways. That is an undisputable testimony to the power of one person simply following God's guidance for caring and teaching others to do the same.

EVERYONE HAS SOMETHING TO OFFER OTHERS

I appreciate Stephen Ministries because it is a ministry of caring that nonprofessional people can do, and we can learn practical tips for caring for others simply by perusing their Web site (www.stephenministries.org). Even if your church is not involved formally with Stephen Ministries, you can still benefit from what they teach. Stephen ministers are trained to simply listen with a caring, nonjudgmental heart during times of need.

Stephen ministers do not heal. They trust God to be the Healer. They share prayer and Scripture when appropriate while respecting the needs of others by building trusting relationships. They are not counselors or therapists. They are not problem solvers or clergy. They are simply everyday people who have a desire to cultivate and use the spiritual gifts they have been blessed with. By doing so they experience great joy as they see God working through them to bring hope and healing to a hurting world, one person at a time.

One woman whose husband died instantly in an accident on his way to work said that seven weeks afterward she was alone visiting his grave when she finally realized he was gone. She fell apart and remembers thinking, "If

I was sick, I'd go to a doctor. If I had a toothache, I'd go to a dentist. I had a spiritual problem, but I didn't know where to go. When I looked across the cemetery, I saw my church in the distance. That's where I went." With the encouragement and support of her Stephen minister, she began to piece her life together again. But her story does not stop there. Having benefited from Stephen Ministries in another congregation, she decided to bring it to her own congregation.

The Stephen Series log (an area on their Web site where people, without solicitation from Stephen Ministries, can post stories about how their lives were affected by this organization) tells the story of a care receiver's journey from brokenness to wholeness through the transforming power of the cross of Jesus. It serves as a simple reminder that it is not the Stephen minister who restores a person to wholeness. Rather, it is only through the cross of Jesus that a person can be made whole. God's love surrounds us and heals us, with the cross of Jesus at the center of His love. We are merely the caregivers, God is the Cure!

SIMPLICITY MADE SIMPLE

Prayerfully **CONSIDER THE POSSIBILITIES**. Seek God's guidance by making prayer an important part of your decision-making process. Clearly, not everyone is gifted for this kind of ministry. If God has impressed your heart with a ministry for caring—then consider Stephen Ministries. You can learn more about them through their Web site at www.stephenministries.org.

Examine your church's mission or vision statement to **SEE IF STEPHEN MINISTRIES WOULD BE AN EFFECTIVE TOOL** for your congregation. They are a nondenominational, nonprofit organization that is now in more than nine thousand congregations from more than one hundred Christian denominations, in all fifty states, nine Canadian provinces and twenty other countries.

Caregivers experience great joy as they see God working through them to **BRING HOPE AND HEALING TO A HURTING PERSON**. The benefits of this spiritual caring are that it provides hope, healing and a new sense of self-worth that only God can bring. Those who care also grow a deeper relationship with the Lord as they experience God's unconditional love for them and those they care for. They also benefit by knowing they are active partners in the mission and ministry of their church. They will find all aspects of their lives enriched by the caregiving skills they learn and practice.

INCLUDE FELLOW CHURCH MEMBERS in your outreaches. As members discover the meaningful ministry of caring, they will want to respond to the call to become more involved. Your church will become a more loving community that is sensitive and responsive to the people's needs for care. As local churches are able to provide more quality devout care, fewer people with needs will slip through the cracks. A caring church ministry is also better equipped to reach out to the unchurched that are hurting and introduce them to the healing power of Jesus.

Lord, I am grateful for those who reach out to the needs of others. Lead me to mentors who can teach me to do the same, and to resources that are available to meet the practical needs of people in our community. I'm willing to get involved, Lord, and ask You to show me the who and how—I'm ready to trust and obey. Amen.

Mentors

The aged women likewise, that they be in behaviour
as becometh holiness, not false accusers, not given to
much wine, teachers of good things.

—TITUS 2:3 (KJV)

My twenty-year-old goddaughter recently moved out into her first apartment. Of course, she was very excited about this new phase of her life. But amid the excitement, the reality of what she could afford, and what she needed, was what you might call a *budget discrepancy*! She needed dishes, but there wasn't any budget for them. We all cleaned out our cupboards searching for the best of the unmatched dishes, cups and saucers, and my friend Patty donated a small four-piece set that was very special. When Patty had moved out on her own after her divorce, a friend gave her this set of dishes—because they had been given to her when she first moved out on her own. These dishes have been passed on from woman to woman several times. The agreement was that if you accept the dishes, you also agree to the obligation to someday pass them on to another woman in need.

Those dishes reminded me how simple it can be for us to support and care for each other—especially women. We are natural caretakers. We share naturally with each other on a deeply personal level. And that makes us natural *mentors*. Yet the word *mentor* scares a lot of women away from pursuing a connection with a teacher or protégé because it sounds so formal—it sounds so corporate. But it doesn't have to be. It can be as simple as responding to a tug on your heartstrings when you meet someone who is taking a journey you have already made.

In the very early stages of my divorce, I was lost. I cried and cried some more. At that point, I was not capable of caring for myself very well. But a friend who had already walked the path of divorce came alongside me and mentored me through the process. Several years later, I was able to do the same for another. And so the caring gets passed on. I have always believed that we have an obligation to help others through experiences that God has already brought us through. Whether it's divorce or cancer or simply helping a young mother adjust to the pressures of her new role. Mentoring is biblical and necessary.

WHATEVER IS GOOD—PASS IT ON

Jesus' whole life was a role model for mentoring. His disciples, by definition, were "learners." If we take what we learn from one woman and pass it along to another we gain wisdom. Robyn Claydon, senior associate for Women in World Evangelism, says, "Mentoring is rather like running an Olympic race. The older, more experienced leaders running the Christian race are—or will be—in the process of handing the baton on to those coming up behind. They don't suddenly hand the baton on, for the other person may not be ready and drop it. For a time, as in the race, one runs alongside the other giving him or her strength and encouragement and handing the baton when they know they are ready. Mentoring is running alongside someone else for as long as it takes."

That is just what my friend did for me during my divorce. She stayed, guided, comforted and prayed, all the time watching and waiting to see how I was responding. As she felt I was ready for the next phase—she would coax me on to getting professional counseling and to finding a lawyer. If she had pushed me too soon, I would have resisted because I just wasn't ready to accept the reality that my marriage was over. I needed grieving time and she knew that because she had been through the same thing. Colossians 4:17 (ESV) says, "See that you fulfill the ministry that you have received in the Lord." I believe that mentoring others through similar life paths is a very significant ministry every disciple can fulfill, irrespective of age or experience. The basic requirements are simply living a life that involves a relationship with God and an ability to listen and respond with sensitivity.

"John Wesley's 'General Rules for Methodist Fellowships'. . . released in 1743 included, 'Watch over one another in love.' This was the key to his success in retaining those who were converted through that revival. In class meetings and one-to-one, they cared for one another." I love the definition Rev. Dr. John Mallison gives for mentoring in his book *Mentoring to Develop Disciples and Leaders*: "It [mentorship] is a dynamic relationship of trust in which one person enables another to maximize the grace of God in his/her life and service. It has a sound biblical and theological basis with Jesus as the ultimate model, retaining all that is consistent with his life and teaching." Maximizing God's grace—that is the perfect definition. We are all so blessed by the grace of God. How could we not share it with others? Clearly, mentoring is not merely a suggestion. It is God's design that each generation should guide the next.

I read a Guideposts story written by Arthur Gordon titled "My Words to Grow On," in which he talks about learning from helpful words or phrases that usually were spoken by older and wiser friends. One friend, Dr. Karl, spoke to him about life's purposes:

> Someone once asked me who of the many people I have interviewed over the years had impressed me most. Not an easy question, but I found my mind going back to a visit I made to the Menninger Foundation in Topeka, Kansas, and the time I spent with Dr. Karl Menninger, considered the dean of American psychiatrists. I felt then that I was in the presence of a towering genius, and nothing since has caused me to change my mind.
>
> I can recall his office vividly—the Navajo rugs on the floor; the Native American artifacts everywhere; Dr. Karl wearing a yellow shirt with turquoise cufflinks, peering at me with eyes that were penetrating and kind.
>
> We were talking about the importance of hope in human affairs. "If you lose all hope," the doctor said, "you stop trying and you stop caring. That won't do. I think each of us is put here to dilute the misery in the world. You may not be able to make a big contribution, but you can make a little one, and you've got to try."
>
> Help dilute the misery in the world. A tremendous challenge and an uncompromising yardstick. It might profit all of

us to think about it at bedtime once in a while. Ask yourself honestly which of your actions during the day came close to fitting that definition. If you can think of a few, sleep soundly.

If not, do not despair. The sun will rise again tomorrow. You will have plenty of opportunities then.

Diluting the misery—what a wonderfully simple way to put it!

SIMPLICITY MADE SIMPLE

Be willing. Remember, the basic requirement for mentoring is only a living relationship with God and an ability to listen and respond with sensitivity. You don't have to be fully mature in all areas of your life. In fact, many mentors actually have a mentor themselves while mentoring others. Serving as an effective mentor simply means that you are open to Christ, learning and growing, and actively pursuing your own maturity. **THE GREATEST GIFT YOU CAN GIVE IS YOURSELF**, especially when given out of the grace of God.

Follow the mentoring agreement. **THE TWO KEY INGREDIENTS** for mentoring to be successful are trust and confidence. Christian mentoring is an ongoing relationship between two people who agree that mentoring is not therapy, counseling or a replacement for mental health care. It is simply a commitment to love and trust God as you demonstrate compassionate caring for the one you are mentoring. If you have endured disappointment, grown in your understanding of God's trustworthiness and sense that God wants you to be a mentor, then seek through prayer His will for your role as a mentor.

MAKE A DIFFERENCE. Today, only about fifty percent of children will grow up in an intact family. Children whose parents divorce have been shown to have higher emotional problems, lower school performance and poorer family economic standing at age sixteen. Statistics show that mentoring makes a difference for these children. In fact, scientifically controlled studies have shown that students involved in mentoring were forty-six percent less likely to begin using drugs, twenty-seven percent less likely to use alcohol, thirty-three percent less likely to engage in violence, and fifty-two percent less likely to skip school. Mentored students also felt more confident about schoolwork and enjoyed better relationships with parents and peers.

Make no excuses. **NO MATTER YOUR AGE OR YOUR LIFE EXPERIENCE—THERE IS SOMEONE WHOM YOU CAN HELP** through mentoring. Think you're too busy? Some of the best mentoring is done by those who are very active. Housebound? Many who are housebound mentor effectively by means of their phones or by inviting others to visit them. Too old? Not at all. Mentoring can be a very fulfilling role for those of mature years, allowing them to grow older as participants rather than spectators.

Life can be hard, but **YOU DON'T HAVE TO GO IT ALONE**. Pray for boldness and courage to take the risk, pushing aside your pride, and ask God to show you who He might have you approach to seek out a relationship—specifically for the purpose of being mentored.

Be flexible. **BE AVAILABLE** and be willing to ask questions. Mentoring is an act of service. Your relationship must be God-honoring and trustworthy. The person you are mentoring must know implicitly that nothing she tells you will ever be taken any further.

Father, I am grateful for those who cared enough
to teach me how to live a better life. I have learned many
great lessons since I have trusted my life to You. I am
willing to pass on to others those words of wisdom and
easier ways to do things. Connect me, Lord, with those who
will benefit from what I have to share. Amen.

Nonjudgmental Caring

"Do not judge, or you too will be judged. For in the same
way you judge others, you will be judged, and with the
measure you use, it will be measured to you."

—MATTHEW 7:1–2 (NIV)

This Scripture that says, "Do not judge, or you too will be judged," is often taken out of context and misused as a way of keeping people from making the necessary moral judgments that wisdom dictates. Sadly, this is particularly true in our culture, where too many individuals seem to think it is impossible to express moral advice and at the same time remain compassionate. Yet, Christ was trying to teach us to do just that—assert right from wrong with compassion.

Jesus clearly warns us not to assume God's prerogative to condemn the guilty, but He also warns us to discern truth from error (Matthew 7:15–23). In fact, Jesus is not opposed to our offering correction, but only against our offering correction in the wrong spirit.

In Matthew 7:5 (NIV), Jesus said, ". . . first take the plank out of your own eye, and then you will see clearly to remove the speck from your brother's eye." Yet, in Matthew 18:15–17, Jesus gives clear instructions that if someone sins against us, we are to go to that person and show him his fault. If he listens to us, great! But if he will not listen, we're to take one or two others along with us. And if he still refuses to listen to the church leadership, we're instructed to simply avoid that person.

God's Word places responsibility on us to be each other's caretaker, even in spiritual matters. Galatians 6:1–5 (NIV) says, "Brothers, if someone is caught in a sin, you who are spiritual should restore him gently. But watch yourself, or you also may be tempted. Carry each other's burdens, and in this way you will fulfill the law of Christ. If anyone thinks he is something when he is nothing, he deceives himself. Each one should test his own actions. Then he can take pride in himself, without comparing himself to somebody else, for each one should carry his own load."

As we read in Matthew 7:3–5, Jesus does not say it is wrong to help a fellow Christian remove the "speck of dust" in his eye, but it is wrong for a person with a "plank" in his own eye to offer help! It is only when we are able to approach another in a meek and self-judging spirit that we can be of help. It is only when we remove the log from our own eye that we have the opportunity and responsibility to help our brothers and sisters remove the specks from theirs.

Understanding this concept and applying it to our lives and the lives of those we see in pain is difficult. Sometimes we feel proud of ourselves instead of compassionate toward those who struggle from the bondage of anger, alcohol, drugs, spousal abuse, money, sex and other addictive behaviors. We look at their lives from a human perspective and miss the reality that it is only by the grace of God that we too are not in the same place.

IT COULD BE US ONE DAY

It is hard not to be self-righteous and make hasty judgments when we *think* we know the answers to another's woes. Someone once said that telling an alcoholic not to drink would be like telling a tuberculosis patient not to cough. It is exactly that kind of judgmental advice that Christ warned against. Jesus wants to slow down our judgments. He wants us to do only the kind of judging that we would be willing to have come back to us.

But having right beliefs about judging is not enough. The Bible commentary at BibleGateway.com puts it this way: "Even if we knew people's hearts, we could not evaluate degrees of personal guilt as if we understood all the genetic and social influences that combine with personal sinful choices in making some people more vulnerable to particular temptations (such as alcohol or spouse abuse) than others. Most important, Jesus warns us that even if we knew people's hearts, we would be in no position to judge unless we had lived sinless lives, never needing God's forgiveness."

Instead, Jesus taught us to pray with humility, realizing that we too have sinned against others, just as they have sinned against us. So how do we help those who are struggling with burdensome issues that are dramatically affecting their lives and the lives of those around them? First, we must learn to love the person despite his or her behavior.

With those needing forgiveness and care who are close to us, we must take a long look at how we ourselves may sometimes, unknowingly, enable their behavior to go on. We must reach out to them. This can be one of the hardest tasks because we need to be able to detach ourselves from the symptoms of their disease—such as abnormal behavior, irresponsibility, lies, cheating and perhaps even stealing. We must be able to recognize these actions as part of their sickness.

We must also resist taking the blame for causing the problem—no matter what they say. We simply must learn to detach lovingly, without anger or resentment. And we must stop reacting to symptoms. Most important, we must reach out to God. Only He can change people. When we reach out to Him, He becomes a Partner that can help us live and act as He would toward others. He is our strength. He gives us perspective. When we rely on Him, answers come. And sometimes those answers involve letting someone else be the instrumental caregiver in our loved ones' lives as Guideposts writer Mary Jane Clark discovered:

> We still receive the monthly newsletter from the church we belonged to some years ago. It's interesting to read of its accomplishments, its concerns and new projects. As I skimmed over the newsletter the other day, my eye was caught by a familiar name, a "Thank you to Mr. and Mrs. ____" for some office equipment they had donated to the church.
>
> When I first heard that name, I was visiting with my friend Pam while our sons played together in her backyard. She told me about Richard, the young man who would be discharged from prison in a few weeks, and who was coming to live with them. Pam's husband Frank, a teacher at the university, had gotten acquainted with Richard through a correspondence course. Over several years their relationship deepened into a genuine friendship.
>
> I remember wondering if Pam and Frank's decision was a good one. We had opened our home to a lot of people over the years, but none of them, as far as we knew, had prison records.

"We realize there are some risks involved," Pam told me. "But we've met Richard. We've asked a lot of questions over there. And most importantly, we feel confident that God wants us to do this thing."

Richard joined the family in their tiny house on Wilson Street. He quickly settled into a job, and it wasn't long before he found his own place to live. We enjoyed seeing Richard's shy smile every Sunday morning. We rejoiced in his milestones: baptism; confirmation and joining the church; his wedding to Sarah. We were invited to the opening night of his art show at a local gallery. Now Richard and Sarah have an established business of their own, and they are contributing members of the local community and the church.

Thank you, Pam and Frank, for the important part you played in helping Richard turn his life around. Thank you for modeling Christ's love in your open home and open hearts. Your example reminds me how quick I am to make judgments about people, and how wrong I can be when I predict someone's future based on the mistakes of the past.

SIMPLICITY MADE SIMPLE

ADMINISTER GRACE. Grace leads to a change of heart, which leads to repentance. And repentance is an awesome and terrifying gift because it forces people to look at themselves honestly and acknowledge their failings. But repentance is also a gift that leads all of us back to the grace of God. It is only when we understand God's grace that we are no longer bound by our past actions. Instead, it is through repentance and grace that we find what God in Christ has done for us. His grace both judges and forgives. His grace includes everyone—all those we find religiously acceptable as well as those we don't! That is the challenge of caring for those in need.

REMOVE THE PLANK FROM YOUR OWN EYE FIRST. This is a straightforward but extremely important verse to follow if you truly want to care for others. For example, if you wanted to help someone with anger, then it would be absolutely necessary for you to have a firm grip on your own anger before you could help the other person. Many people have problems with anger but sometimes it actually becomes a part of who they are. It is important to remember that anger is simply an emotion, but it is also a choice of the human mind; anger is not an involuntary reaction, it is directed by our thoughts. Sadly, anger is also the most powerful human emotion that there is. People use it to cover feelings of hurt, embarrassment, powerlessness, worry and fear. It can become such a part of their personality that letting go of it leaves them feeling defenseless. They will only change when they believe the change is warranted.

SPEAK COMPASSIONATELY WITH RESPECT, PATIENCE AND A KIND HEART. Let them be heard. This is the most coveted thing you can do for people. They simply need to know that someone cares for them and is there to listen to their wants and really understand their needs.

JUDGE YOURSELF—ESPECIALLY YOUR COMMUNICATION AND LISTENING SKILLS. Have you tailored your skills to the needs of the people you are trying to help? Even distraught people want to be needed and understood. Consider your own behavior. This is most helpful if it is a family member whom you are trying to help, because we often learn behavior from other family members. Each of us is ultimately responsible for our own behavior, and we must examine ourselves to see if we are adding frustration to their lives and inadvertently pushing them over the edge.

GIVE PRACTICAL HELP TOO. I recently heard Suze Orman, the financial advice guru, on a television show. She was speaking with a young man who was struggling financially. He was a pocketbook designer and had been fortunate enough to find a job with one of the top designers in New York City. He shared an apartment with a couple of long-time friends. He had been trying to manage his money for years. As a result, he no longer had a credit card or even a checking account. He was living on a cash-only basis. That sounded good, yet each month he ran short and did not have the cash for the rent. His mom usually "lent" him the money, knowing full well that he would not be able to pay it back. Suze Orman asked him details about his life and found that his social life consisted of going to nightclubs three times a week. She suggested that he stop going one night a week to the clubs and put that cash into one of his beautifully designed handbags. A simple but effective savings plan. She also suggested that he start paying back his mother a little each month. Why was this so important? Because Mom was actually enabling her son to continue in his ways. It kept her in the place of righteous authority and at the same time supported his bad habits.

Father, when I examine my heart and behavior,
I always find areas that need more of Your grace
to help me to do what is right. I confess my sins
and ask that You cleanse me from all that does not bring
You honor and glory. From a right heart, full of grace,
let me simply be a blessing in the lives of others. Amen.

Conclusion

Three times Christ asked Simon Peter, "Do you love me . . . ?" And each time Peter answered, "Yes, Lord; you know that I love you." The Lord responded, "Tend my sheep" (John 21:15–17, RSV). To be a follower of Christ requires that we care for others. And there is certainly no lack of people to care for. Sometimes the caring is easy, as simple as making an encouraging phone call, and other times it's more difficult; the lonely, the aged, the weak or the troubled, these are much harder to care for. We cannot just kiss away their sorrows, but we can do something—even if it's simply holding a hand and praying.

Remember, prayer should be the beginning of all our caring. We should pray that God would guide us to the "sheep" He wants us to care for. Then we should pray that He would prepare our hearts and our minds to "authentically" be there for them.

Finally, pray for God to be with you. Our loving God cares for us all. He doesn't just call on you to care, but He empowers you to care as well. When you offer a caring touch or a loving glance, you are demonstrating His love to a hurting world and that can make all the difference to someone in need.

Notes

Part One—Caring Is the Heartbeat of Love

1. Patricia E. Deegan, PhD, "Recovery as a Self-Directed Process of Healing and Transformation" (2001), www.intentionalcare.org.

2. Walter Bruegemann, "Shalom," www.eco-justice.org.

Part Two—Caring Is a State of Mind

3. C. H. Spurgeon, "The Compassion of Jesus," a sermon, December 24, 1914—delivered at the Metropolitan Tabernacle, Newington in London, www.abideinchrist.com.

4. Marilyn Schlitz, "The Love Study," California Pacific Medical Center, November/ December 2003, www.spiritualityhealth.com.

Part Four—Caring Is an Act of Grace

5. Barbara Deane, *Caring for Your Aging Parents* (Colorado Springs, Colorado: NavPress, 1992), 20.

6. Dawn J. Lipthrott, LCSW, adapted from "Help with Intense Feelings, Recurring Thoughts, and Grieving," www.relationshipjourney.com.

Part Five—Caring Opens the Windows of Heaven

7. "Overflow," words and music by Matt Goss, copyright 2004 Matt Goss Music, used by permission.